Discover . . .

- how panic attacks are related to body chemistry
- which foods can help prevent panic attacks—and which can contribute to them
- mental tricks and techniques that can short-circuit mounting anxiety as soon as it occurs—sometimes in as little as six seconds
- and more

When you learn the facts about panic attacks, you can attack back. This guide—with a seven-step program, nutrition and fitness facts, and encouraging true stories—can help.

Shirley Swede is the founder of PASS-Group, Inc., a telephone counseling organization for panic attack sufferers. **Seymour Sheppard Jaffe, M.D.,** now retired, is a former clinical member of the American Academy of Behavioral Medicine.

"*The Panic Attack Recovery Book* . . . offers practical, straightforward, easily implemented and effective measures to overcome panic. The book is well written, and conveys reasonable optimism that the person who suffers panic attacks can take control of his/her life."—I. M. Hulicka, Ph.D., Distinguished Professor (Emeritus), State University of New York

THE
PANIC ATTACK
RECOVERY BOOK

REVISED AND UPDATED

SHIRLEY SWEDE AND
SEYMOUR SHEPPARD JAFFE, M.D.

NEW AMERICAN LIBRARY

NAL Books
Published by New American Library, a division of
Penguin Putnam Inc., 375 Hudson Street,
New York, New York 10014, U.S.A.
Penguin Books Ltd, 27 Wrights Lane,
London W8 5TZ, England
Penguin Books Australia Ltd, Ringwood,
Victoria, Australia
Penguin Books Canada Ltd, 10 Alcorn Avenue,
Toronto, Ontario, Canada M4V 3B2
Penguin Books (N.Z.) Ltd, 182–190 Wairau Road,
Auckland 10, New Zealand

Penguin Books Ltd, Registered Offices:
Harmondsworth, Middlesex, England

Published by New American Library, a division of Penguin Putnam Inc. Previously appeared in Plume Trade Paperback and Signet Mass Market editions.

First New American Library Printing, September 2000
1   3   5   7   9   10   8   6   4   2

Copyright © Shirley Swede, 1987, 2000

All rights reserved

⨂ REGISTERED TRADEMARK—MARCA REGISTRADA

LIBRARY OF CONGRESS CATALOGING-IN-PUBLICATION DATA:

Swede, Shirley.
The panic attack recovery book: revised and updated / Shirley Swede
and Seymour Sheppard Jaffe.
p.   cm.
Includes index.
ISBN 0-451-20043-8 (alk. paper)
1. Panic attacks—Popular works.   2. Self-help techniques.   I. Jaffe, Seymour.   II. Title.

RC535.S94   2000
616.8'5223—dc21
00-35500

Printed in the United States of America
Set in New Baskerville
Designed by Leonard Telesca

This book is dedicated to
the late Dr. Claire Weekes
and
to the many wonderful people we have met through
the PASS-Group program. Without them, this
book could not have been written.

A special thanks to: Carole Hall,
editor of the first edition of our book;
Louise Gault, our agent;
and Ellen Edwards, editor of the revised edition.

Contents

Preface

When new medications that were specific for blocking panic attacks first came out, they were hailed as a panacea because they allowed a person to move about more freely. He could go back again and again to those places he feared—without having to worry about a panic attack—until the cycle of sensitization–fear–avoidance was broken.

However well this strategy worked for many patients, it wasn't without a price. First of all, some had unpleasant side effects from the medication. Second, the relapse rate after the medication was stopped was very high; the panic attacks returned in a great many cases.*

Yet many doctors today are still using medication to block the panic attacks prior to exposure therapy simply because they know of no alternative. They are not aware that the panic attacks can be eliminated and the body's chemistry corrected *without resorting to drugs.*

This is why I'm so pleased to introduce you to the program in this book. It presents a viable alternative to medica-

---

*Pecknold, J. C. and Swinson, R. P. "Taper withdrawal studies with Alprazolam in patients with panic disorder and agoraphobia." *Psychopharmacology Bulletin, 1986,* vol. 22: 173–76.
Noyes, R. Jr., Chaudry, D. R., Domingo, D. V. "Pharmacologic treatment of phobic disorders." *J Clinical Psychiatry,* September 1986, 47: 445–52.

tion for panic attack sufferers. This program helps eliminate panic attacks without the possibly hazardous effects of drugs.

I'm a physician; I've been trained in medicine, so I'm not opposed to drugs per se. I prescribe them when I have to. But if a person can recover without drugs—through *natural* means—isn't that much to be preferred?

—SEYMOUR SHEPPARD JAFFE, M.D.

Introduction

Dear Reader,

Let me introduce myself. My name is Shirley Anna Swede, and I'm the founder of PASS-Group.

PASS-Group stands for "Panic Attack Sufferers' Support Group," and also for "We were helped—now we PASS along this help to others." Here's how this organization was started.

For many years I had a problem with recurrent panic attacks. But I found a way to recover. I knew there were a great many people who were suffering as I once did, and I wanted to help them. At that time, the problem of recurrent panic attacks wasn't as well-known among the medical profession as it is today, nor was it as widely publicized.

One day I put a small notice in a neighborhood newspaper. Some of the people who responded were stuck at home, so I began to make "house calls." When it became impossible for me to make personal home visits to all the people asking for help, I began to encourage them over the phone.

Out of that beginning grew the idea of a telephone counseling service for panic attack sufferers. Not a hot line but a three-month course that emphasized the preventive aspects of my methods. In 1981, PASS-Group, Inc., was officially incorporated. Two friends (also recovered panic attack sufferers, whom I'd helped) and I became its first counselors.

This book tells all about the PASS program and about some of the men and women who have participated in it. So this isn't my story alone; it's *our* story.

If you are like most of us who have had panic attacks, you probably feel you are alone and there is no one who could possibly understand how you feel or what you go through. But you're wrong. There is no symptom, no matter how bizarre and frightening it may be to you, that we have not experienced too.

You may feel you are weak to let this thing get the better of you. Perhaps you think you might fight it off and not "let" yourself be this way. Well, that isn't true, either. Sometimes just getting through a bad day takes more courage than anyone who has never experienced a panic attack can imagine.

As far as fighting, you have been fighting. You just haven't had the right weapons. Tensing up, clenching your teeth and telling yourself, "Oh, no, this time I'm not going to let it happen," only adds fuel to the fire.

So what do you do? What are the weapons? If you're doing this to yourself, how do you stop? This book will provide you with answers.

Remember, no matter how hopeless you may feel your case may be, it isn't. You are now part of a network of people who do understand your problem and what you are going through. And we know there is a cure for you, just as there was for us.

The edition of *The Panic Attack Recovery Book* that you're reading now is a revised, updated version of a book I originally wrote in 1987. This edition contains more information, more practical ways to implement the program. I can only add that if you try this comprehensive approach—and stay with it—the results will amaze you.

Yes, we at PASS-Group continue to do one-on-one counseling. If you'd like to participate—if you'd like to have a mentor, someone to discuss your progress with—just let us know. We'll send you an application and some information about our telephone counseling program.

Best wishes and good luck.

Sincerely,
Shirley Anna Swede

PART I

THE FEAR THAT COMES FROM WITHIN

CHAPTER 1

Panic Attacks: What Are They?

Panic attacks are the most common—and the most treatable—"mental health problem" in this country.

But what exactly is a panic attack?

Simply put, it's a short burst of intense fear; a feeling that "the sky is falling down." Here, for example, is how one woman describes a panic attack:

> All of a sudden, for no apparent reason, you're overwhelmed by a feeling of impending doom. Like something terrible is about to happen. You feel you've got to get out of there *real quick*. Your heart pounds and you feel like you can't breathe, so you try and *make* yourself breathe—and then you start to hyperventilate. Your hands tremble and your legs feel like they're made of Jell-O. All sorts of things go through your mind—like maybe you're having a heart attack. Or maybe you're going crazy. You don't know *what* it could be—and it's so scary.

Probably the scariest part is that you *know* there's nothing in the environment that's threatening or dangerous. No one is coming at you with a gun. So you conclude maybe you're having a heart attack (because your heart is going ninety miles an hour!). Or maybe you've "lost it" and gone crazy.

You're afraid if anyone knew, they'd come and lock you up—so you keep it to yourself. It becomes your Great Big Secret.

And you learn to avoid. "Maybe if I don't go there, it won't happen." You often end up inventing excuses *why* you can't go there. Because how do you explain it to an "outsider"? This is how the pattern of avoidance is set up—and in time it becomes a habit. Yet this is a logical sequence of events that can happen to any thinking, sensitive person.

The late Dr. Claire Weekes, an Australian physician and pioneer in the treatment of panic attacks, wrote in her book *Simple Effective Treatment of Agoraphobia* (Hawthorne, 1976), "Sensitization can be shocking and confidence quickly shaken. One does not have to be a dependent type—as I have heard agoraphobics* described—to be so affected."

But what's behind it? Why do these panic attacks come "out of the blue" (as so many describe it)?

The answer is, they don't. Typically, this is how the panic attacks start:

1. There is a stress "overload" for a period of time prior to the onset of the panic attack. (It could be physical stress—like an operation, difficult childbirth, etc.; or it could be emotional stress—loss of a job, a divorce, etc.)
2. The person is in a "run-down" condition—i.e., poorly nourished and not physically fit for the amount of stress load he or she is carrying.

These two conditions, taken together, can temporarily alter the body's chemistry, as well as the nervous system's sensitivity to stimuli, and bring about a host of unpleasant symptoms that we commonly associate with fear: Heart palpitations, lightheadedness, shakiness, a feeling of "not really being there."

*"Agoraphobia" refers to the habit of avoiding certain places or situations because of the fear of having a panic attack there. "Panic disorder" means having recurrent panic attacks. These two terms are often used interchangeably.

Then a third factor comes into play: If the person starts to focus on these symptoms and worry about them, naturally they become more pronounced.

Many normal people experience some degree of panic from time to time. It might occur during a period of hormonal change such as the onset of puberty or menopause, when studying too hard, or when dieting too strenuously.

But if the person doesn't pay too much attention to these feelings and symptoms, the body eventually "rights" itself. Time, they say, is a great healer, and whatever stress the person is undergoing sooner or later passes. Or the person somehow learns to adjust. But some people continually ruminate about their symptoms. They don't take proper care of their bodies. They just run from doctor to doctor, looking for a magic cure. If a person worries in secret that the panic attacks are a sure sign of impending insanity or serious illness, then the panic attacks keep coming. Because the person is not giving his body a chance to recover.

Some time ago, I (SS)* met a woman who told me her story. About fifteen years ago, she said, she was in a supermarket, shopping. All of a sudden, her knees got weak, her hands started to tremble, and her heart pounded. She left the wagon of groceries and ran out of the store. The next time she was in the supermarket, the same thing happened, only worse.

That very evening, she went to see her doctor, who happened to be an old family friend. He examined her carefully and said, "Betty, there's nothing the matter with you. You're just run-down and you need a rest." He prescribed a good diet, some vitamins, exercise—and he sent her home. He also advised her not to go to crowded supermarkets, but to do her shopping when it was not so busy—until she felt better.

She followed his advice, and pretty soon things were back to normal. Eventually, she was able to do her shopping even

*SS refers to author Shirley Swede; SSJ refers to author Seymour Sheppard Jaffe.

during crowded times. And she never experienced these episodes again. Now, she jogs, eats well, and enjoys her job.

Yet had her doctor not been as wise and understanding as he was, she would—in all likelihood—have been in treatment for years.

You're probably asking: "If the cure is that simple, then how come so many people suffer? And how come panic attacks can last twenty, thirty—even more—years?"

The answer is that getting into trouble is easier than getting out of it.

When a person is living under constant fear and stress, his body's chemistry changes. The body speeds up the production of stress chemicals. The body, you see, is doing its best to keep up with the demands made upon it. But the more stress chemicals you produce, the greater your body's need for oxygen, for certain nutrients—vitamins, minerals, etc. If you're too busy worrying and not eating properly, where are these nutrients going to come from? When poor health habits (coupled with poor attitude) become firmly entrenched, they tend to perpetuate themselves. It becomes a vicious cycle. You become trapped unless you take steps to reverse this process.

In this book we present a recovery program that will show you how to begin to take those steps.

Agoraphobia (Panic Disorder) and "Simple" Fears

It's important to make a distinction between panic disorder and the so-called simple phobias—fear of cats, of thunder, etc. These simple phobias are "outside" fears; panic disorder, on the other hand, is an endogenous fear, meaning that it comes from within.

Dr. Claire Weekes was one of the first to recognize this fact—when many others didn't. She talked about the fear of fear within oneself. You are not afraid of the actual places, you are afraid you will be unable to cope and what it may lead to. Quite a different matter, Weekes added, from the fear of something "out there."

Thus, panic disorder might cover a whole range of fears—including closed-in places, heights, bridges, driving, public speaking, etc.—*if* the fear stems from the same source: Namely, the fear of having a panic attack in that place or situation.

Why is this distinction important? Because the origin in each case is different. A simple fear—the fear of dogs, for example—might be the result of having been bitten by a dog or unduly cautioned about dangerous dogs. The treatment of simple phobias is pretty straightforward: You recondition the person's reaction through a series of gradual exposures, coupled with relaxation techniques. The first "exposure" might be a picture of a dog. Later on, the treatment progresses to seeing a small dog at a safe distance, then a bigger dog, and so on, until a person's tolerance to dogs is increased.

But endogenous fear is something else. It's a fear that wells up by itself from something inside. It belongs in a different category and requires a different treatment.

Take a person who's afraid to go down Main Street because he once had a panic attack there. You can't show him a picture of houses and explain that there's really no danger, that the street is safe. He* *knows* there's no danger there. He's just afraid those terrible feelings will come over him again once he's back on the street. So it's not a question of taking him there gradually. He has to be adequately prepared; he has to know about the countermeasures he can take to prevent the panic attacks. Because if he goes to Main Street without this preparation and gets a full-blown panic attack there, he's "sensitizing" himself all over again!

---

*We really mean "he or she"; but for the sake of brevity, we use the traditional "he."

So exposure therapy alone isn't enough. This concept—that there must be an adjunct to the exposure therapy, *something to relieve the panic attacks first*—is widely recognized and accepted, but most therapists are using medication for this purpose.

Our program presents an alternative. In a great majority of cases, you can get rid of the panic attacks without the use of drugs. This is borne out not only by our observations but also by the experiences of other therapists in the field who are using essentially the same methods we're using.

If you're already on medication to help block the panic attacks, this program can be used as a means of weaning yourself off the medication, or as a backup when you eventually stop the medication. However, we caution you *not* to stop the drugs abruptly, which may precipitate the panic attacks again, or even to cut down the dosage on your own. *You should only change your medication under your doctor's guidance and supervision.*

CHAPTER 2

How the Nervous System Works

In order to gain a better understanding of the nature and origin of panic attacks, it's important to have a basic idea of how the nervous system works. This chapter will give you a nontechnical explanation of some of the forces involved.

Your Nervous System

The nervous system—indeed, the entire body—is constantly adapting to new situations. There is a constant interplay of forces; nothing is ever static. In this way nature maintains a balance—or homeostasis—in the ever-changing environment that is your body.

Your nervous system is divided into two basic categories: the autonomic and the voluntary nervous systems. Your voluntary nervous system is under your direct control, as when you raise your hand. Your autonomic nervous system is *not* under direct control. It is subdivided into the sympathetic and the parasympathetic systems. You would think that the sympathetic one is the calmer of the two because the name suggests something calm and gentle. But it's actually the opposite: The sympathetic nervous system is the one that's aroused when we're angry or frightened. The parasympathetic is the one that calms, that inhibits. In health, both systems operate together in harmony.

The Brain

The brain is roughly divided into three parts: the "logical brain" or outer brain; the "reptilian" or very primitive brain that lies low-down and "sits" over the spinal cord; and the "emotional brain," the interbrain, that lies between the two. In actuality, of course, the functions of the brain are not so neatly divided. All functions are integrated, and there are countless intricate connections among the nerve cells.

The Body's Sentry—the Hypothalamus

In a sense, the hypothalamus heads the autonomic nervous system. It is located in the emotional brain. It is not a large structure (only 3 percent of the total brain weight). Its influence, however, is enormous. Dr. Gustav Eckstein of Harvard calls it the pilot. But it's usually referred to as the body's sentry.

The hypothalamus sounds the alarm to alert the body in case of danger. It sends a message to the pituitary gland—which, in turn, alerts the adrenal glands—and adrenaline (epinephrine) is sent charging into the bloodstream, mobilizing the body.

We all know, of course, that anything that spells danger in the outside environment—like someone pointing a gun at you—will make the sentry sound the alarm. But it's often overlooked that the sentry stands guard over the inner environment, too. In other words, the sentry can pick up clues from the body as well as the mind. Here's how the sentry might become aroused.

The mind: Whenever you believe (it need not necessarily be true) that your existence, your ego, your self-esteem, or your integrity is being threatened—an alarm goes off. It's your perception that determines your reaction. Thus, panic attacks can be triggered by *thoughts.*

The body: The triggering factor might be an overactive thyroid, where "all systems go." Or it might even be a severe allergy. Obviously, you should have a complete physical checkup by your doctor to rule out any frank physical cause. However, one of the most common causes for an inner environment emergency is a blood sugar level that fluctuates too much, that habitually drops too rapidly.

The brain, in order to function normally, needs a constant supply of sugar (glucose) and oxygen. It must have both, because the sugar can only be "burned" (metabolized) in the presence of oxygen; together, they make the energy the cell needs. (It's like when you put gasoline into your car. The fuel is "burned" if oxygen is present, and that's what makes the energy that drives your car.) If not enough sugar is present, there's a problem, and if not enough oxygen is present, there's a problem. Brain cell metabolism can't proceed—and this is a cause for alarm. The sentry is alerted, and through the chain of command mentioned before, adrenaline is released into the bloodstream.

Now, some of the effects of adrenaline (and there are many) are these: It increases the breathing rate and heart rate, and it makes the body release some of its stored sugar into the bloodstream. The blood sugar level rises; the brain gets what it needs—and it can continue to function.

Yet the side effect of having a lot of adrenaline in the system is the sensation of fear, apprehension—even panic (that's why they call it a panic attack!). As you look around and you see nothing in your environment that's particularly threatening, you might—erroneously—conclude that maybe this means (a) you're dying; (b) you're going crazy; or (c) something really horrible must be going on in your "subconscious." Naturally, this causes even more apprehension and anxiety. (The sentry is now *really* alarmed!) And that means even more fear and more adrenaline.

Yet the panic attack has served a purpose. Looking at it that way, the panic attack may well be a defense mechanism

of the body. It may be the by-product of an emergency measure in order to get more blood-carrying glucose and oxygen
to the brain. The increase in heart rate, breathing, sugar in
the blood—all have the effect of rushing to the brain the
material it needs to survive. It's almost like a game of chess:
You can lose all your pieces, but as long as the king is saved,
you're still in the game. As far as your body is concerned, the
brain is king!

There are other indications that a panic attack may be
Nature's way of getting more sugar into the bloodstream
on an emergency basis. High levels of growth hormones
have been found in the bloodstream during a panic attack.
Growth hormones—aside from helping you grow—also prevent sugar from being deposited in the liver (the major
storehouse for sugar). Not only that, but the growth hormone decreases the rate at which sugar is metabolized. The
net effect is to increase the available sugar in the bloodstream.

"Well, then," you may say, "if my brain needs more sugar,
that's great. Because I do eat a lot of sugar."

No, it isn't great. Because—paradoxically—the more sugar
you eat, the *less* your brain gets! Here's why:

Sugar Overload

Everybody's blood sugar level fluctuates somewhat,
depending on what you've eaten and when—and the amount
of stress or excitement you have. (That's because stress and
excitement use up a lot of energy, and sugar supplies energy.)
In some people, though, these fluctuations are more erratic;
there are greater "highs" and lower "lows."

What makes it this way? And how does it relate to panic
attacks? Let's review what we know about the so-called sugar
cycle.

All cells use sugar (carbohydrates) for energy. There are

two types of sugar: simple sugar (as in the sugar bowl) and complex sugar (as in vegetables and whole grains). Simple sugar is ready to be used "as is" by the body. It doesn't have to be broken down first, because it's already in simple form. Complex sugar, on the other hand, must be broken down before it can be used—and this is done in a series of steps. When you eat foods high in simple sugar ("junk foods"), you're dumping a lot of sugar in all at once. Since it doesn't have to be broken down first, it enters the bloodstream right away—and the sugar level rises too steeply. Now, insulin has to come in to take away the sugar and lead it to the cells. What happens with many people—especially those who have been eating large amounts of sugar for a long period of time—is that the body adapts itself to the greater sugar intake by making it easier for the insulin to be released. The pancreas is "trained" to respond more rapidly, and with greater enthusiasm than necessary. The more insulin that comes in, the more sugar is taken away—and there is a sharper drop in the blood sugar level. At this point, the person begins to feel hungry (usually for sugar foods) and shaky. The body, you see, is calling for more sugar for energy.

If a person hasn't eaten in a while, the body has to dip into its reserves to get the sugar. But in order for the sugar to be released, adrenaline has to come into the picture, because adrenaline holds the key to the sugar storehouses.

If a person has been under stress for a long period of time, he has—unwittingly, perhaps, but similarly—trained his adrenal glands to release a lot of adrenaline, the "fight-or-flight" hormone. Yes, it brings the other side effects of adrenaline: rapid heartbeat, increased breathing, and the intense desire to run, to flee!

As far as blood sugar is concerned, insulin and adrenaline are on opposites sides of a seesaw: Insulin takes away the sugar; adrenaline puts it back.

Under normal conditions, when the person is on a fairly

good diet and there's no stress overload, everything works smoothly: sugar (i.e., complex sugar) comes in; insulin takes it away. Then more sugar comes in (if not immediately available from the diet, then from the body's storehouses), and the cycle continues. But it's the combination of stress *and* poor diet (rich in sugar, low in vital nutrients) that plays such havoc with the system. The body simply can't handle all that sugar.

Craving for Sugar

When the body has a requirement for a certain nutrient, it often sends out some sort of message. For example, if you eat a lot of salty foods, you become thirsty. So you drink water, the salt is diluted, and equilibrium is restored.

"So if I crave coffee and cake," you may ask, "doesn't it mean I need sugar?" Yes, you probably do. It usually means the blood sugar level has dropped too low. (Stress uses up a lot of energy!) But here's the catch: If you eat simple sugar (or a heavy meal) you're throwing in a lot of sugar all at once, causing the insulin to come out full force. The more insulin comes in, the more adrenaline has to come in—to balance it out. So it creates a vicious cycle.

This, we think, is why many people fall into the trap of eating sweets (or taking a drink) whenever they feel shaky, tired, depressed, or under stress. (Has this been your pattern, too?) If you eat something with a lot of sugar in it and drink coffee, you feel better right away. Do you see why? The quick energy of the simple sugar and caffeine entered your bloodstream and gave you a temporary lift. If this had happened to you, you probably concluded (logically) that cake, candy, or coffee help you cope. Yet, as you see, although it helps in the short run, in the long run it only makes the problem worse. Because the lift drops with a thud—later. So you're only perpetuating those highs and lows.

The way out of this dilemma is to help stabilize the blood

sugar level and keep it on a more even keel. You quiet down the overenthusiastic hormonal responses (the production of insulin and adrenaline) by reducing the amount of stress in your life; by eating a good diet; and by eating small, frequent meals. You substitute complex sugar for simple sugar. Complex sugar takes about four times as long to absorb, so the rise is more gradual, and hence the tapering off is also more gradual.

People react differently to a drop in sugar in the blood-stream. Some will get symptoms, others won't. Out of a group of one hundred "normal" people, maybe about twenty-five will have a "low blood sugar," but only three will develop symptoms, according to a statement by the American Diabetes Association. And even the same individual will respond differently on separate occasions. So it's difficult to establish hard-and-fast rules.

Should you take a glucose tolerance test for hypoglycemia? We don't think it's necessary. (Why bother if the tests are inconclusive anyway?) But if you want to, you can do your own testing. When you feel shaky, drink a small glass of orange juice. If you feel better in a few minutes, well, that's probably hypoglycemia.

Hyperventilation

Hyperventilation is the medical term for rapid breathing. When one breathes this way deliberately, it causes temporary symptoms, which can be very frightening to someone who doesn't understand what's happening. The symptoms are: dizziness and lightheadedness; a strong feeling of apprehension; the lips may feel numb; hands and feet lose their coordination; the pulse speeds up; and the heart begins to pound. Thus, every day, in hospital emergency rooms all over the country, people are brought in, hyperventilating, in a state of terror, in what they perceive to be their last moments on earth—only to be told by a doctor that they're in perfect health and just "suffering from nerves."

Breathing, as we all know, brings in oxygen and removes the waste products. But the respiratory system engages in still another very important function: that of regulating the acid-base balance of the body fluids.

Acid and base (alkaline) are chemical opposites. The normal body fluids are slightly on the alkaline side, and they must be maintained that way, within a certain narrow range. The body regulates this balance by withholding or releasing just the right amount of acidity.* How does the body get rid of the excess acid? By throwing it off in the urine—and in the breath.

When you exhale, you give off carbon dioxide and water. Before it becomes carbon dioxide, it's carbonic acid (an *acid*). When you overbreathe (hyperventilate), you're releasing the carbonic acid, so you're turning your body's chemistry more toward the alkaline side. Sometimes overbreathing has to be induced by the automatic nervous system—as, for example, when you have a high fever. During high fever, metabolism increases and there are more (acid) end products of metabolism. The body has to get rid of the excess acid, so the breathing is automatically increased. This corrects the too-high-acid concentration in the blood.

But when over-breathing is done *deliberately*—and many nervous people have a habit of doing this without even realizing it—you are turning your body fluids toward the alkaline side for no good reason. This causes an imbalance between the acid and the base that wasn't there before!

When the body goes too far on the alkaline side, it brings on the symptoms we just mentioned. But remember, these symptoms—however unpleasant—are not dangerous. And they are only temporary. The reason they occur is that when

---

*We can almost hear you saying, "But what if it doesn't?" Don't worry. The body has several back-up systems for this; it's fail-safe.

the blood becomes more alkaline, the blood vessels automatically constrict. This limits the amount of oxygen and glucose going to the brain.

These symptoms occur when *anyone* overbreathes; one doesn't have to be a "nervous person" to be so affected (although, if one is nervous, the symptoms can occur more quickly). A number of medical investigators have purposely induced hyperventilation in themselves in order to study its effects on the body. The famous scientist J. B. S. Haldane did this. In an essay called "On Being One's Own Rabbit," he describes how he got "violent pins-and-needles" in his hands, feet, and face after breathing deeply and rapidly for two to three minutes. He also writes how he once had "continuous spasms" in his hands and face that lasted one and a half hours after a period of self-induced hyperventilation.

Normally, breathing is slow and even. But when there's not enough oxygen in the environment—or if your body's oxygen-carrying capacity is diminished, for whatever reason—the carbon dioxide level in the bloodstream rises. This rise in carbon dioxide triggers the breathing mechanism. In other words, *the body itself initiates the increase in breathing* in order to compensate for the deficit in oxygen.

For example, if you're in a room where there's a higher level of carbon dioxide—let's say, in a room that is poorly ventilated, with a lot of people in it; or if you're in a greenhouse where the carbon dioxide is kept artificially high for the benefit of the plants—your breathing rate is apt to increase. (Remember, it's the carbon dioxide that triggers the breathing mechanism; when it reaches a certain point, the body says, "OK, breathe faster.") A nonphobic person would just take this increased breathing in stride and think nothing of it. But a panic-prone person—an individual who looks inward too much, ready to focus on anything he perceives to be "abnormal"—would be more sensitive to the fact that he is breathing a little faster, and this may have a snowballing effect. The thought: "Oh, my goodness, what's happening to me now—am I starting to get a panic attack again?!" produces fear and an even greater increase in breathing.

Once you understand this, we hope you can at least remain calm *mentally,* even though your breathing may be temporarily increased. We hope you will realize that this is merely the body's attempt to bring in more oxygen and that you won't become unnecessarily frightened by the increased breathing. Because the fear itself might lead to panting and overbreathing, with the attendant temporary disruption of the body's normal biochemistry. (Later on, we'll talk more about the breathing, and show you how you can use it as a means of relaxing yourself.)

Sometimes a little thing like a stuffy nose can bring on a "big" problem with panic attacks. You get panicky feelings when you can't breathe and then you worry why this is happening to you. But *anyone* who feels he can't breathe will react with panic! So when you sense your nasal passages becoming clogged—due to allergies, perhaps—the simple but obvious remedy is to open your mouth a little and breathe. (Later you can look into the problem of allergies.)

Some people, because of prolonged tension and stress, feel their chest muscles are "too tight." So they conclude they have to push their breathing along—otherwise, they think, they may stop breathing altogether. But this is an incorrect assumption. Remember, no one ever committed suicide by holding his breath! You may hold your breath voluntarily until you're literally blue in the face and faint. But eventually you'll breathe. Why? Because carbon dioxide will accumulate in the bloodstream, and when it reaches a certain level it will stimulate the respiratory center in the brain and you'll resume breathing. That's the miracle of the body's biochemistry at work.

Here's an interesting fact about breathing: For some people, the more attention they pay to their breathing, the more irregular it becomes. When I (SS) was in nursing school, we had to check each other's pulse and respiration.

As soon as we knew our breathing was being observed, the normal rhythm became disturbed. This happened to many of us in the class; it was hard to get an accurate measurement.

So you have to allow your body to do its job; you have to trust your body more. It knows what it's doing. After all, it's been breathing since you were born.

Sodium Lactate Infusion

Back in 1967, doctors at the Washington University School of Medicine demonstrated that it was possible to regularly induce a panic attack in patients who had previously complained of spontaneous panic attacks. When the doctors administered sodium lactate intravenously, the patient would experience all the agonizing symptoms of a panic attack. This seldom happened to others, who might only experience mild symptoms, such as numbness and/or muscle tremors (sodium lactate is an alkalizing agent).

Since sodium lactate is a normal by-product of cell metabolism, we can infer that the people who respond with panic might simply be more sensitive to the buildup of this chemical. Or that sodium lactate isn't being removed from the system at the proper rate. Or that the level of sodium lactate is already high in a person who is subject to panic attacks, and that this additional infusion merely throws him over the edge, setting the stage for a full-blown panic attack.

But why, you ask, would the sodium lactate level be high in the first place?

Let's talk for a moment about muscle activity. Muscles are normally slightly contracted. This is called muscle tone. During sleep, when the body is relaxed, there is very little muscle tone. But during waking hours there is always some muscle contraction going on. (Otherwise, how would you be able to sit or stand?) A very nervous person, one who jumps at the slightest noise, would have a great deal more muscle tone, because his muscles would be doing a lot more contracting; they'd all be keyed up. Now, in order to perform, muscles need oxygen. So it stands to reason that a person who is very tense most of the time will use up more oxygen than someone who is relatively relaxed.

Whenever muscles are made to work (i.e., to contract) without enough oxygen being present, a chemical called lactic acid starts to collect around the muscles. Muscles don't like to have lactic acid hanging around; it literally cramps their style. It makes them ache and feel fatigued. So the body has to get rid of the lactic acid. How? By breaking it down, ultimately into carbon dioxide and water. But in the process of breaking it down chemically, sodium lactate is produced. Therefore, if you have a lot of lactic acid to begin with, isn't it reasonable to suppose that there would be a lot of sodium lactate as well, since the latter represents a chemical reaction produced by the breakdown of lactic acid?

So what it boils down to is this: Science has finally confirmed that nervous, sensitive people are more likely to get panic attacks.

And yet, understanding the underlying chemistry gives us a better handle on the problem:

1. You can increase your body's ability to process oxygen more efficiently (making the most of each breath, so to speak).
2. You can teach your body to conserve oxygen by decreasing your body's need for oxygen.
3. You can enhance your body's ability to get rid of excess lactic acid.

Fortunately, all of the above can be achieved through the integrated steps presented in this program. Since each helps the other, the *combined* approach is far more effective than any single method alone.

The Fear Center in the Brain

Experiments with laboratory animals show that when an electrode (an electrical stimulus) is applied to a certain part of the hypothalamus, the animal reacts with acute fear or rage. More recently, a series of experiments were performed at another brain site called the locus coeruleus (suh-rool-ee-us), which we'll call the LC. The LC is much smaller than the hypothalamus. But it also has a very important role, since virtually all important brain structures, including the hypothalamus, are connected to it in some way.

When Eugene Redmond of Yale wired the brains of monkeys and electrically shocked them at the LC point, the monkeys exhibited their equivalent of what in humans would have been a panic attack. So it may very well be that the first panic-button-pusher is the LC—and the panic may be brought about by nerves firing off at this location instead of—or along with—the hypothalamus. But whatever the final research shows, the theoretical concept is still the same: The feeling of panic is being triggered by bursts of electricity deep within the brain.

The EEG that we use to measure brain activity—although it can pick up signals emanating from the *outer* layers of the brain—is not sensitive enough to pick up signals that come from within the deeper, interior parts of the brain. Such signals are weak to begin with, and, in addition, must pass through many layers of tissue and bone before they reach the "outside" where they can be measured. Thus, direct evidence of electrical misbehavior in the LC or hypothalamus is lacking; however, we infer—as we always do from analogous experiments with animals—that this is indeed what is happening in the human brain.

But it must also be understood that these local sites, however interesting they are to the researcher, to you, to us, are not isolated sites in the sense that they signal, "Aha, we have found the culprit!" Their influence extends, by means of a complicated network, to all major parts of the brain. And, of course, the brain is connected to the body. So we always have to keep an eye on the total picture—instead of just a tiny part.

Does this mean that the LC has "usurped" the hypothalamus's role as the body's sentry? Some researchers think so. They've called the LC the alarm system of the brain. But whether it's the LC or the hypothalamus is, for our purposes, relatively unimportant. The basic concept—namely that there is in the brain some coordinating mechanism that functions as a guardian or sentry that can trigger the fight-or-flight response—is still the same.

The LC also seems to act as a regulating device that can turn up or turn down all stimuli—much like the knob on a radio that controls the volume.

The Endorphins

Additional studies of the LC reveal that it is richly endowed with opiate receptors. Opiate receptors are nerve cell receptors that only accept chemicals resembling opium and opium derivatives like morphine. This was an astounding discovery. How could the body know that opium would ever be used? The discovery led to an intensive search for some naturally occurring substances that would chemically resemble the structure of opium. And finally such substances were found. They were named endorphins.

Here's what the endorphins do. They diminish pain, anxiety, and fear; enhance the immune system of the body (hence the ability to withstand stress); and lower the threshold for pleasure—which means it makes it easier for any pleasurable stimuli to get through.

The endorphin and opiate receptors are chemically complementary. One fits into the other, like a key in a lock. So, to put it in the very simplest of terms, the endorphins plug up the holes in the fear center of the brain, so the fear doesn't come out.

The discovery that there is a fear center in the brain and that the fear center is richly supplied with opiate receptors is a very significant one, because this information now gives us yet another handle, a way of dealing with the fear response. It shows that there is a way of turning down the volume, so to speak, of a "hyper" nervous system—through the increased production of endorphins.

CHAPTER 3

Conditions Associated with Panic Disorder

A number of popular theories link certain conditions and/ or symptoms with panic disorder. Let's examine some of them and see how they relate to panic attacks.

Mitral Valve Prolapse (MVP)

Among those who suffer from panic disorder, the percentage who also have MVP is significantly higher than among the general population. More women than men have MVP. It seems to be inherited.

How is MVP, an anatomical imperfection in the heart, related to panic attacks?

Let's review the anatomy. The heart is divided into four chambers: left, right, upper, and lower. The mitral valve separates the heart's upper and lower chambers on the left side of the heart. The blood passes the mitral valve as it moves from the upper chamber to the lower. Normally, this passage is a one-way route: The valve opens up, allows the blood to flow through, then closes tightly to prevent a backflow. However, if there's a slight defect in the valve so it can't close tightly, a small amount of blood may seep back through, to the upper chamber. This condition is generally considered benign; the imperfection in the valve might be of no more significance than imperfectly spaced teeth. A statement by the New York Heart Association is very reassuring: The condition does not seem to be a cause of heart attacks.

You can readily see that at times, especially during stress, not enough blood may be getting through to the brain fast enough. This could cause a temporary dizziness or feeling of lightheadedness. The body, in an effort to send more blood to the brain, speeds up the heart rate. But the mind, at this point, might also signal a red alert: What person wouldn't be frightened if he thinks he's having a heart attack?

If you're worried about possible heart problems, for your own peace of mind, you should see your doctor.

We want to add this, though. The heart is a muscle. And, like any muscle in the body, it can be strengthened through exercise. As the heart gets stronger, the heart can afford to slow down, because now the heart is able to squeeze more blood through with every beat, every thump. And this means more oxygen and more food to all the cells, including, of course, the brain cells. A deconditioned heart, on the other hand—one that's weak through lack of exercise—must keep beating faster and faster, especially during stress. The heart just doesn't have the power to squeeze through, with one swoosh, any great amount of blood, so it has to do it with many tiny beats to keep up. Obviously, a stronger heart would ensure a better blood supply and diminish the episodes of dizziness.

Problems of the Inner Ear

Another condition with a high correlation to panic attacks is trouble with the inner ear. That's where the body's balancing mechanism lies. There's always fluid there, and when we move or turn our heads, the fluid moves, too, to maintain its level position (it's like tilting a glass of water). From this information, the sensitive nerve-endings in that area pick up the message regarding the body's position and relay it to the brain. The brain then sends messages to the various muscles—and that's how the body maintains its balance.

However, if there's some swelling in the inner ear (due to infection, allergy, and so forth), the fluid increases and presses against sensitive nerves. The message gets garbled; it's as if you were on the high seas. This brings on a giddiness and nausea that can range from a slight feeling of being off-balance to the sensation of seeing the room spinning around like a merry-go-round—only it's not so merry.

The ground may appear to be wavy or as if it's buckling under. There may be episodes of lightheadedness, dizziness, feeling unsteady on the feet, or having the impression of tilting to one side while walking. These sensations can trigger panic attacks in sensitive individuals—especially if you don't know what's happening and assume the worst. True, light-headedness can be a manifestation or symptom of the panic attack itself, but it can also be the cause of it. Remember we spoke earlier of how the sentry stands guard over the inner environment, too? A sense of disequilibrium in the body—particularly if it occurs suddenly—can make that sentry sound the alarm.

Sometimes this condition is referred to as Ménière's syndrome, but, actually, Ménière's is characterized by three conditions: dizziness, ringing in the ears, and hearing loss.

Elevators, escalators, cars, buses, planes, and boats are common places for a panic attack. Getting panic attacks in places associated with motion should raise the suspicion of an inner-ear involvement. Consult an ear-nose-and-throat specialist (otolaryngologist) to rule out or confirm this condition. But don't worry—it's treatable. A salt-free diet is usually recommended, with or without medication.

Premenstrual Syndrome

During the premenstrual period, many women suffer from a combination of symptoms caused by water retention. The excess fluid also irritates the nervous system, which accounts for the feelings of inner shakiness, a tendency to fly off the handle, and panic attacks, if one is predisposed to having them. The blood sugar level tends to be more unstable at this time, too, so many women get strong cravings for sweets just before their period. What you can do is have more complex carbohydrates at this time—and pay even closer attention to your diet and vitamin supplements. You can also take frequent, brief exercise breaks.

The standard non-drug treatment of PMS—a good diet, exercise, stress-reduction, salt-restriction, and so on—is exactly what we will be recommending for panic attack recovery.

Enzyme Impairment

Besides increased adrenaline and insulin production, some researchers have found, in their studies of a group of panic attack sufferers, some impairment of enzyme activity related to carbohydrate metabolism (i.e., the way the body burns sugar).

What are enzymes? They're substances that make chemical reactions possible; they're catalysts. Enzymes need certain vitamins to help them do their job (vitamins are often called co-enzymes). Without vitamins in the right amounts, the enzymes can't work properly. As we've already said, one of the by-products of carbohydrate metabolism is lactic acid. Therefore, if metabolism doesn't proceed normally, lactic acid will tend to accumulate. And this can trigger panic attacks in susceptible people.

Why might this enzyme system become impaired? It might be the result of years of poor diet (i.e., eating foods whose vitamins and other nutrients have been removed through commercial processing) and/or a higher inborn requirement for certain vitamins. Whatever the cause, this condition does seem to be reversible. Common sense would dictate that the aim of the therapy could be to correct the underlying malfunctioning enzyme activity, through good nutrition and vitamin supplementation.

In our experience, large doses are not needed—probably because we use a total, holistic approach and because each facet of the program helps restore proper balance and health. In any case, megadoses of vitamins (or any other nutrient) should *not* be taken without adequate supervision by a professional who is knowledgeable in nutrition. In megadoses, vitamins act like drugs.

A Chemical Imbalance

There used to be—and still is, in certain quarters—a controversy about whether panic attacks are the result of emotional factors or whether they're the result of a chemical imbalance. Those who favor the emotional factors want to treat panic disorder with behavior modification; those who favor the physical component want to treat it with drugs.

Anything that stimulates the overproduction of hormones (adrenaline, insulin, enzymes, etc.) creates an imbalance, a disturbance in the body's chemistry. We're all chemical factories, in a sense. You literally couldn't lift a finger without a chemical reaction taking place! Foods are chemicals, too. Think about it. These entities—plants, animals, eggs, fish— were once alive. And now, when you eat them, they are mechanically and chemically broken down by your body for your own use. The energy locked in those foods is released and passed on to you when you eat them.

So if you're not getting the right foods that your body needs, won't there be a chemical imbalance? If your lactate level builds up too much (because you're too tense all the time or because your carbohydrates aren't being metabolized properly or because your oxygen-carrying capacity is underdeveloped)—isn't there a chemical imbalance? If you (or anyone else) start to overbreathe and the body's acid-base balance is temporarily disturbed—that's a chemical imbalance, too, isn't it? If your body is producing too many stress chemicals because you're overworked—or because you're thinking of danger all the time—what does that do to your body's chemistry?

Yet, many people assume when they hear the phrase chemical imbalance that there is some missing-link chemical—and if only they could get their hands on it, they'd be cured.

Sure, certain drugs have been found to be helpful in blocking the panic. However, with drugs you always have to consider the possibility of undesirable side effects. Some of these drugs are relatively new, so no one knows what the long-term side effects might be. In addition, when you stop the drugs, the panic attacks may return.

Certainly, it is far better to correct the chemical imbalance through natural means—through diet, exercise, stress management, and a positive attitude. These are the methods we use in our program, with excellent results.

Now, we're not taking the position that medication should never be used. But it should be used as a last resort, not as a first choice. If there are other options available, why take unnecessary medication?

Why Are There More Women Sufferers?

Why are there so many more women who suffer from agoraphobia? Dr. Claire Weekes reported that less than 10 percent of her patients were men. Yet in our experience, some years later, closer to 30 percent of the people we have helped are men. We attribute this increase to the newer attitudes about male/female roles. Men today are not as reluctant to admit they're afraid. They're a lot more open about it. We even feel that many more men have panic attacks but mask them with alcohol. The physical reason often given for alcoholism is a recurrent lowering of the blood sugar level—certainly something very similar to what seems to be happening in panic disorder.

There may be other reasons why women are especially prone to agoraphobia. Girls generally have a more receptive, waiting attitude than boys. If there's danger out there, they're not as apt to run to meet it head on. (As Gloria Steinem once remarked, "Women don't have to prove anything.") So they can more easily fall into the habit of avoiding if they choose to emphasize the "dangerous" aspect of going out. Boys, on the other hand, have a different orientation. Testosterone, the male hormone, creates in young men much more of a drive to go out, to do, to meet danger. Boys also tend to be more active physically. In young women, poor nutrition and poor physical conditioning can have a bad effect on the glandular system, particularly the menstrual cycle. As we have seen, this can cause swelling in the brain and other tissues prior to menstruation, making the panic attacks more likely to come at this time.

So all these factors may weight the balance "in favor" of women.

Yet it is interesting to note, in passing, that when the German physician Dr. C. Westphal coined the term agoraphobia in 1871, he did so after he encountered in his practice three patients who were afraid to go to the center of town—and all three patients were men!

CHAPTER 4

How to Prepare Yourself for the Program

You have just seen how a number of factors, working together, can stir up the nervous system into an upward spiral of chaos. By using the same principle—a number of factors, all working together—you can reverse this spiral. You can make it go in the opposite direction.

How do you go about calming a nervous system that you can't reach directly, that's not under voluntary control? The answer, of course, is that you have to do it indirectly.

The PASS-Group program of recovery consists of the following seven components:

1. Diet
2. Relaxation
3. Exercise
4. The Right Attitude
5. Imagination
6. Social Support
7. Spiritual Values

These components, or steps, are aspects of your life that you do have control of. By working on them you will be able to calm your nervous system and cure your panic disorder.

A client once told me that she sees the problem of panic attacks as a round circle, like a pie. Each part of the program (the seven steps), represents a slice of the pie. So when you eat right, you take away a piece. When you change your attitude, that's another slice gone. When you exercise, another piece. Pretty soon nothing is left of the pie—and the panic attacks are gone!

We are often asked: Do I work on all seven steps at the same time? Although we have presented the seven components of the program as individual steps, each in a separate chapter of the book, we suggest that you work on them all more or less simultaneously. Read through the entire book before you begin so that you understand everything that is involved. Then make a start in one area, take a small step in another, and so on. I (SS) usually tell my clients to begin with diet—for most people it's the easiest place to start.

We ask that you do not start going out to those places and situations you fear the most until you have been working on the seven steps long enough to feel physically stronger, calmer, more adequate. Naturally, this timespan varies with each individual, but in most cases it's about six to eight weeks. If you had a broken leg, you wouldn't run right away, would you? So you have to allow time for your body/mind to heal also.

Alleviate Stress

The panic attacks are stress-related, so as you begin the seven steps of the program, anything you can do to alleviate the stresses in your life will be of great help. Most of us, thank goodness, don't have to face life-or-death emergencies on a daily basis. Most often, it's the accumulation of the little stresses that gets us down. That's why it's important to give thought to how your daily life is structured.

Think of your day-to-day activities as a continuum that goes from one extreme to the other:

No Activity	Too Much Activity
Boring, stifling	Frantic, agitated, distraught

The Fear That Comes from Within   33

Either extreme—too much as well as too little activity—is very stressful to the human body. Obviously, most of us would be more comfortable somewhere around the center—but whether it's a little more to the right or left of that center is strictly an individual preference.

The idea, of course, is to work out a balance that's right for you. Where would you feel more comfortable?

If you have a strenuous job either at home with small children or in the business world, it's important to balance it with quiet, restful activities at certain times during the day. You shouldn't save the pent-up frustrations and then go on a two-week-long holiday. Instead, balance your activities on a daily basis. If you don't have the time, then make the time. It's your health and happiness that are at stake.

Say, for example, you're a free-lance writer, working at home. Writing is lonely; it's also sedentary work. So, in order to create a balance, you have to find company. You have to do some activity that involves walking, exercise, and so on. A mini-vacation for you might be to close shop and go visit a friend. Or go jogging in the park for a while with a friend. If, on the other hand, you have a busy workday—seeing a lot of people or going to meetings, for example—a mini-vacation for you might be to take time out and curl up with a good book, work on a stamp collection, or paint. Being with people all day long, adjusting to novel situations or getting a lot of input, can be very tiring day after day. Your mind needs rest and relief.

Pleasure Island

One of the most effective ways to relieve daily stress is to create "pleasure islands" during the day. Some little activity that you enjoy doing—even if only for a few moments at a time.

For example, for me (SS), reading is a great pleasure. I

don't have time to sit down with a book for an hour, so I do what I call "snatch reading." I usually have a variety of books on hand, and every time I sit down for a snack (I eat often!) I read. I also love to chat with friends, write letters, play with my dog, watch a good show on TV. These are the little, everyday pleasures I'm talking about.

You have to create for yourself little islands of pleasure— *especially* when you're surrounded by a sea of stress—because unrelieved stress and tension, without respite, cannot do you or your family any good.

Tuning Out

Many people have a habit of turning on the radio for the news and weather first thing in the morning. This is a very bad practice. The news is always bad, and when you hear it in the morning, it sets your mood for the day. If you must listen to something in the morning, tape some nice music and listen to that. Or something uplifting and cheerful. (You can always find out about the weather by dialing a certain number—ask your local information operator.)

Some people ask: "But if I don't listen to the news, how would I know what's going on in the world?" There are billions of humans in the world today. That means billions of events, good and bad, are happening all over the world. But the media people select only the news they want you to hear. They don't tell you that a woman on your block had a wonderful evening with friends. They don't tell you that so-and-so finally got his long-awaited promotion. They don't tell you anything about ordinary people, who are just living their lives.

And yet many people think they know "everything" because they read the papers and listen to the news . . . or, conversely, that they won't know "anything" if they stop listening.

Those of us who are prone to panic attacks are highly

susceptible to our environment—good *or* bad. We're highly suggestible. That's why we benefit so much by feeding our minds positive thoughts instead of negative thoughts.

An Old Wound

Sometimes there's a lot of stress in your present life because you focus too much attention on an old, hurtful event that may have happened long ago. It becomes like a scab that's constantly being picked on. You don't give your wound a chance to heal.

In her book *Peace from Nervous Suffering* (Hawthorne, 1972), Dr. Claire Weekes suggested four "principles" which work well here—face; accept; float (in the sense of: ease up a little, let go, don't hold on to the hurt so tightly); and let time pass. We might just add one more principle—allow other interests, other friends, other experiences, to enter your life. Those beneficial influences can be the very ointment you need for your wound, to help it heal.

You're far less apt to be resentful, less inclined to ponder the injustices done to you, when your life is filled with good things.

The Worry Hour

Many people are champion worriers. They've had so much time to practice! What I tell them is this: Set aside a certain time to worry. I call it the worry hour. Do all your worrying only during that time. Leave the rest of the day free for other pursuits. Whenever a particular worry comes to mind, you don't have to say, "Oh, I mustn't think of it, I mustn't have that stress," etc. You can say to yourself, "I'll think about it later. At 4 P.M." (But don't be surprised if you can't keep your mind on your worry for that whole hour!)

Look for the Good

You've heard this expression many times before: "It's the little things in life that count." So why not try this: For one month, keep a "Diary of Beautiful Things." Record the little things you see every day that are beautiful, that reach out to you. For example, the way the sun shines on a piece of glass, the color of a flower, the way someone smiles at you, etc. Learn to find pleasure in the commonplace things around you.

Sometimes, when we're confronted by ordinary stressful life situations and personality clashes, it may seem as if there's nothing we can ever do to change it. And yet, a positive way of thinking and looking for the good can often work wonders.

For example, here's what one client told us:

> I used to have a lot of stress on my job. And mainly it was because I was working next to this girl I didn't like. I just couldn't stand her. I used to be so irritated by everything she said and did. But then one day—I don't know how this idea came to me, but I thought of this: No one can be all bad or all good. So I said to myself, there must be something good about this person. And I began to look for it. I began to search out the good qualities. And I did find several things about her that I liked. So I kept concentrating on those things. And then a miracle happened. This girl became a lot more friendly towards me! I guess she sensed that I liked her more, so she began to like me. And so our friendship started to grow.
>
> Now things are so much better on the job. It's a pleasure coming in to work in the morning because I don't have all this negativity around me anymore. I feel better. And I feel a little proud of myself, too. Because I know I was the one who took the initiative to change things.

Having a Goal

Everyone needs a goal, something to strive for. To accomplish. To look forward to. I've (SSJ) seen people in nursing homes languish and deteriorate rapidly—not only because of their age—but because they had nothing to look forward to, nothing to work toward. Everything was done for them; all they had to do was eat and sleep. People need more than that. The human being was designed to exert himself on his behalf, to overcome obstacles, to solve problems. This is good stress, as Dr. Hans Selye, a world-renowned researcher on stress, would have said.

What are some of your goals? Would you like to start a business of your own? Would you like to finish your schooling? Do you have some unfinished business that you'd like to take care of?

Life Thoughts

We all know it's important to develop a more cheerful attitude and to dwell more on the cup being half-full instead of half-empty.

But this is not to say that you must never, ever ponder the sadness in life. These thoughts come to any thinking, sensitive person from time to time. They're part of life. But it's important to realize that this is what it means to be a human being, and that you were not singled out by Providence to be the only person in the world to suffer.

You may remember the old tale about a young woman who lost her newborn son. Her grief was so great that she came to a wise man and begged him to give her an instant cure for her sorrow. The wise man told her she would have to wear, for only one day, the hair-ribbons of a woman who had never grieved. Although she searched everywhere, she could never find such a woman. At last she realized that her troubles were not so very different from anyone else's. Her sorrow lifted when she knew she was not alone.

I once read, a long time ago in one of Pearl S. Buck's books, about a young handmaiden who falls in love with her master's son. She knows full well he can never marry her, and the thought saddens her. She begins to ask herself many questions. She wonders: Is life meant to be sad or happy? She concludes that life is inherently sad; that one can never fulfill all one's desires. But, paradoxically, this thought gives her contentment. She knows she's not the only one who has to suffer.

Sometimes clients tell me they're afraid of dying. (I answer, I'm not so crazy about it myself.) But very often the fear of dying masks an emptiness in life. Psychologist Lawrence LeShan, who did a lot of research on the reactions of terminally ill patients, once told the story of a woman he visited in the hospital. This patient was dying of cancer, and while he was interviewing her, she burst into tears. He assumed this was because she was dying and he tried to comfort her. "No," she said, "I'm not crying because I'm going to die soon. I'm crying because I never lived!"

When you have a reason to live, when you have a task that you want very much to accomplish, when you can hardly wait for a new day to dawn so you can go about your work, the fear of dying falls away.

Dr. Rochelle Myers, a well-known California psychologist, once said, "Most people tiptoe through life trying to reach death safely." They're so overcautious that they don't really live.

Don't let this happen to you.

Seven Anti-stress Tips

1. Don't waste time trying to change somebody. It doesn't work. The only person you can change is yourself.

2. Do one thing at a time. Doing several things at once may be a source of pride, but it is also a source of stress.

3. Maintain a variety of interests, and friends, so when things go wrong in one area, you always have another.

4. If you have a particularly vexing problem to solve, it's very helpful to write it out. The very act of having to put it down on paper helps to clarify your thoughts. And once the problem is identified, it becomes easier to solve: "A problem well-stated is a problem half-solved."

   When you have the problem written out, list all your options. First—do it right off the top of your head, without being judgmental about whether each option will work or not. After you have written as many options as you can think of, go back and write your comments about each one. After your evaluation, select the one that's best. Sometimes, though, none of the options are very palatable. In that case, you strike out those you absolutely don't want—and work with what's left.

5. Another method of problem-solving (once the problem is identified) is to let your subconscious do the work. With this method, you don't try to solve the problem; you only go about getting the facts. You just fill your mind with all sorts of facts you can dig up that relate (directly or indirectly) to the problem. Then, one day—when you least expect it (i.e., when your mind is resting lightly on other things)—a solution may suddenly present itself.

   If no answer comes, maybe you're asking the wrong question. There are some questions that cannot be answered (like the "Why me?" question). So, restate the question; try to see it from a different angle.

6. Get in the habit of breaking up problems into smaller, more manageable pieces. Remember: "One step is enough for me."

7. Get involved in creative work—something that will occupy your imagination to the fullest and make you jump out of bed in the morning, eager to start your day.

Remember, when you're in better physical shape, when you're better nourished and no longer run-down, when your body has been buoyed up by a positive attitude, then you are better able to tolerate the stresses of life.

Listening to Your Doctor

As we mentioned earlier, occasional panic attacks are common. They can happen to almost anyone when we're over-tired, overstressed, and run-down. But an occasional panic attack isn't a sickness. Dr. David H. Barlow, Professor of Psychology and Director of The Center for Anxiety and Related Disorders at Boston University, once made this statement at a phobia conference: "In any given year," he said, "probably up to 30 to 40 percent of the population have panic attacks."

What perpetuates the attacks? What keeps them going? Why are so many people suffering?

There is a constellation of factors at work here: There's usually a lifestyle or environment that leads to isolation and preoccupation with the Self. This intensifies and feeds on any hypochondriac tendencies—that is, a penchant for listening in to bodily functions. It's true that when a person is under stress *and* run-down (in other words, when the parasympathetic nervous system is temporarily subdued and the sympathetic nervous system takes over), bodily functions *are* more evident. The stress chemicals that are being manufactured more abundantly activate the nerve endings in various organs in the body. Thus, heart sounds seem louder, the rumbling in the intestines becomes magnified, and so on. So, in a sense, you can't help but notice these things and become concerned. All we can say is this: Let your doctor be your guide. If he says you're healthy, believe it. If your doctor assures you that no, you don't have heart trouble; no, you don't have a brain tumor; no, there's nothing the matter with your throat, believe it. As you follow the program, as you learn to relax more easily, your nervous system will regain its balance and these symptoms will subside.

Letting Go of Being Perfect

Then there is the matter of wanting to be perfect, another common trait among people who suffer from recurrent panic attacks. In this context, perfection means expecting the body/mind to function faultlessly all the time, so any deviation from the norm becomes a cause for alarm. This quest for perfection becomes an additional source of stress when it overflows into other areas (as it usually does). For example, a person always wants things to be just so, and becomes angry and frustrated when they're not. He may expect family and friends to be perfect also. He may hold back from entering situations where a panic attack might be embarrassing ("What if I make a fool of myself?"). Meaning: How can I show all these people that I'm not perfect? The result of this unrealistic and rigid expectation is a poor self-image, which obviously leads to even more stress.

Some researchers even believe that the striving for perfection (and the constant disappointments) are at the root of the emotional aspects of panic disorder. So it's certainly worth asking yourself: Why strive for something that may be causing harm?

Remember, we're not saying you shouldn't strive for excellence. But there's a difference between striving for perfection and striving for excellence. If you strive for perfection, you berate yourself if things aren't perfect. If you strive for excellence and things aren't perfect—you *don't* berate yourself. You simply correct the error the next time. You're willing to learn from experience, but you don't put yourself down.

The Fear of Going Crazy

So many people who suffer from panic attacks secretly fear they're going crazy. They fear they'll run around screaming and tear their clothes off in public or throw their kids out the window. They're sure that when their anxiety reaches a certain level, they'll crack up and carry out these dreaded deeds. Yet, as Dr. Manuel D. Zane, a well-known researcher on panic disorder, once quipped, "If you don't think a lot of crazy things, you're not in this world." It's natural for the mind to wander into a labyrinth of crazy thoughts when it is overtaxed and the body is run-down.

One day, I was talking to a new client and she said, "I can go anywhere in my own town, but as soon as I try to go to the next town, I get those terrible feelings. I see something awful happening to me. Like I get into an accident. Or the car breaks down. Or somebody is trying to break into my car. [Wouldn't anybody be frightened by such vivid images?] I *know* I shouldn't think of these things," she continued, "and *I try so hard not to.* But I can't help it. They just come to me."

"Suppose," I said to her, "I tell you *not* to think of a white elephant for the next five minutes. Don't, under any circumstances, in any shape or form, think of a white elephant . . . What comes to your mind?" She paused and I could "hear" her smile over the phone. "A white elephant," she replied. If you try very hard *not* to think crazy thoughts, that's practically a guarantee that they'll come. It's a paradox: The more you try *not* to think of something, the more it clings to you. (It's often said that the best way to remember something is to try very hard to forget it.) This woman tried so hard not to worry that she ended up worrying even more!

People under great stress may *think* a lot of crazy things, but that doesn't mean they're going to do anything about it; thinking and doing are two separate issues. The cases you read about in the paper, where someone runs amok, are *not* applicable to you, the panic attack sufferer. Those people have serious mental illnesses of a *psychotic* nature. Psychosis is something else entirely. Psychosis does not *ever* turn into anxiety disorder or a neurosis. These are two separate categories.

Dr. Richard O. Anderson, a psychiatrist, once told me that in order to let this idea sink in with his patients, he asks them this question: "How long can a person have pneumonia before it turns into lung cancer?" The correct answer, of course, is never; they're two separate problems. But some patients will answer, "six months." Or "a year." So he has another question up his sleeve. "How long does it take," he asks, "for a dog to turn into a cat?" At this point, the patient usually begins to smile; he gets the point.

Never Say "I'm Phobic"

Many people use the term "phobic" in describing themselves. They'll say, "I'm phobic" or "I'm agoraphobic." Or they'll refer to the panic attacks as "my" agoraphobia.

After the deluge of publicity on agoraphobia, many were so relieved to know that—finally—"it" has a name. Yet we say this: Don't get so hung up on a name that you identify too closely with it. Once you give yourself a label, you box yourself into a certain category, a certain mind-set. It becomes a self-fulfilling prophecy and it makes it difficult for you to change. You expect to act a certain way, so you do act a certain way. But if you free yourself from the negative label and think of yourself as being in a state of transition (which you are), you're in a much better position to experiment, to try new things. If you keep referring to it as "my" agoraphobia, it'll begin to sound like an affectionate term—and you won't want to part with it!

First Fear and Second Fear

One of the most important contributions in the management of panic disorder was made by Dr. Claire Weekes when she theorized that the panic attack actually comes in two stages. She calls these stages First Fear and Second Fear.

By First Fear, she means the sudden fear that comes unbidden—out of the blue. Second Fear is your reaction to it. It's what you tell yourself about it. It's characterized by self-sentences like: "Oh, my goodness, not again . . . !"; "Oh, this is terrible—I'm surely dying this time . . . !"; "Oh, why is all this happening to me . . . ?!"; "It'll just keep getting worse and worse, and never stop . . ."

Why is this such an important observation? Because in breaking up the problem into two stages, it becomes much more manageable. You can then begin to deal with each of the components as separate issues.

Many people believe that First Fear can be stopped with nothing less than very powerful drugs. But, in our experience, this is not so. There *are* ways to stop or prevent First Fear.

Let's quickly review: As we've said, the panic attacks are initially brought about under the following circumstances:

1. The (susceptible) person has been under stress for a long period of time (before the panic attacks begin).
2. The (susceptible) person has been in a run-down condition (resulting from poor health habits) and is therefore unable to handle that stress load.

But when you raise your level of health—and, at the same time, you decrease the stresses in your life (either by changing the situation or by changing your attitude toward the situation), First Fear diminishes in frequency and intensity—or it disappears altogether.

So you *do* have control of First Fear. (You control it through the voluntary choices you make regarding your lifestyle.)

Therefore, you needn't fear the panic attacks as much— because the panic attacks will, in almost all cases (i.e., if they're still around), become mere shadows of their former selves.

Yes, shock is a very powerful learning tool. That's why you've learned to avoid certain places and situations. That's why when Dr. Weekes says to accept the shock and "let the panic come and do its worst," it's very hard not to flinch! But what we're telling you is that if you've begun following our program, the shock *now,* even if it does come, will, in all probability *not* be as strong as it used to be—and you can handle it. It takes—what? A few seconds? A minute? A few minutes? The shock waves die down on their own.

In *Simple Effective Treatment of Agoraphobia,* Dr. Weekes writes: ". . . [The agoraphobic] should be taught that panic can come only in a wave and must always die down if he but waits and does not fall into the trap of stoking his fires with Second Fear . . . [Without Second Fear] the panic *will not mount.*"

This is most reassuring: "The panic will not mount." Excellent. Well, then, if the panic will not mount—if the worst has *already* happened—what is there to be afraid of?

You can readily see that whenever you add Second Fear, you only intensify First Fear. It's like standing near a quiet pond and throwing in a pebble. You watch the ripples spread—then grow fainter and fainter—until they all disappear and the pond is calm again. But if you keep on throwing in more pebbles, how can it quiet down?

PART II

THE SEVEN-STEP PROGRAM

CHAPTER 5

Step 1: Diet

"Many people think they can just eat any old thing and they're not going to suffer from it. But the laws of Nature set up certain rules and regulations that we have to follow if we want to stay healthy."

—*Helen Conway*, Nutritionist,
Department of Health,
City of New York

Dr. Michael Lesser, a prominent psychiatrist specializing in nutritional medicine, made a revealing statement about nutrition and panic attacks. Here's what he said:

Ninety-two percent of the patients that come to see me with symptoms such as anxiety, depression, fatigue, rapid heart palpitations, fearfulness, trembling, etc., had abnormalities in their blood sugar tests when I administered a five- or six-hour fasting glucose tolerance test to them.

This has led me to draw the conclusion that a blood sugar abnormality is a physiological correlate of the neurotic symptoms. And that if a person is exhibiting symptoms of mental distress of a neurotic character, then it behooves the physician to look into their blood sugar, because very often they'll find there is a blood sugar abnormality. In fact, I find it practically to be the rule. And it may be that the quickest way to treat that person is to deal with that blood sugar abnormality. I'm not saying that the blood sugar abnormality causes the neurosis, nor am I saying that the neurosis causes the blood sugar abnormality. I prefer to think of the individual as a holistic creature, and the blood sugar pattern is simply a reflection of the disturbance in that individual throughout his whole system.

However, I do think that in treating the blood sugar problem, you can often get a very quick response and improvement in that person's health and aid them with their symptoms. Sometimes you can get a complete clearing of their symptoms. Sometimes you can provide that individual with enough energy so that he can go ahead and tackle the important psychological difficulties that he has.

Diet and Resistance to Stress

If you own a dog or a cat, you've no doubt been asked by the vet what you're feeding your pet. Yet people are seldom asked by their doctors what their diet consists of. This never fails to astonish us. After all, even in ancient times many suspected a close link between diet and a person's health. "You are what you eat" is an old proverb. Scientific research and common sense observations have established such a link on numerous occasions. Here are just a few examples.

World War I was fought mainly by soldiers lying in front-line trenches. The stresses on these men must truly have been almost beyond endurance. The trenches were continuously being shelled. There was no retreat (if you retreated, you got court-martialed and shot!). Moving forward or backward, either way, death waited. Under those circumstances, is it any wonder so many men became, as they called it then, "shellshocked"? The nervous system simply can't handle such enormous stress.

But here's a curious thing: The American soldiers had far more shellshock casualties than the British. Yet they faced the same stresses at the front. So why the difference? It was a puzzle until someone suggested it might have been the difference in diet. The English soldiers were fed "bullybeef"— canned meat. The Americans were plied with doughnuts and coffee (hence the name "doughboys").

In World War II, during the London Blitz, doctors reported far fewer "nervous complaints" than before the war. There was a drastic change in the society at that time. The stress of being under intermittent air attack was "offset" by the vastly increased spirit of comradery that marked that period. Everyone was in it together: "Thumbs up!" People slept in air-raid shelters and sang songs. The newly arrived Yanks injected a certain joie de vivre. The Londoners' diet was markedly different, as well. Sugar was virtually impossible to obtain. People ate the vegetables they grew in their own "victory gardens." But after the war, when things went back to life-as-usual, the incidence of nervous and emotional disorders rose again to prewar levels.

A study carried out through Johns Hopkins University involved young children in India—those who were well nourished and those who weren't. The malnourished children were not as adventurous. They were reluctant to explore their environment. They only wanted to stay close to mother. They suffered from what the doctors called separation anxiety, which makes sense from Nature's point of view. To explore the environment takes a great expenditure of energy. But with limited resources, isn't it more important to conserve energy? After all, you can't afford to waste it. Your reluctance to leave your safe world and go out into the wide world may also relate to your nutritional condition.

But, you may say, how come I'm getting panic attacks

when many people eat worse than I do, and they don't get panic attacks at all?

That's a fair question. The point is we all have different tolerances for stress, and we're not all affected the same way. Some people get ulcers under stress. Some get panic attacks. The person suffering from panic attacks is already in a run-down condition. In order to pull himself out of this condition, his diet has to be more than just passable. An ordinary diet isn't good enough.

Moreoever, those who suffer from recurrent panic attacks seem to have a higher inborn requirement for certain essential nutrients and for oxygen. Under stress, this simply becomes much more manifest. Why is this so? Because under stress, the metabolism quickens. The body has to make a greater effort at adjustment; more coping mechanisms are utilized. If a lot of energy is expended, more energy has to be generated. As we pointed out, this means an increased need for oxygen, glucose, and whatever else the cell needs.

When everything is going smoothly, when there's no special stress, you may be able to get by. But once there's added stress, there may be a problem. It's like a bridge: when there's only foot traffic, any old bridge will do. But when heavy trucks and cars have to cross, that bridge better be made stronger.

Some Dietary Guidelines

Here are some general dietary guidelines. But before making any changes in your diet, check with your doctor. This is especially important if you're taking MAO Inhibitors.

1. *Increase your intake of fruits and vegetables* (with emphasis on the vegetables). They're packed with nutrients,

they're rich in fiber (which animal products can't give you), and they have amazing disease-fighting properties. That's why the American Heart Association, the American Cancer Society, the American Dietetic Association, etc., all tell us, "Eat at least five a day!" (They mean in total: three vegetables + two fruits, etc.)

2. *Eat whole grains*—they're rich in B-Complex and other vital nutrients (the milling process removes over 75 percent of these nutrients!).

3. *Eat more foods from the bean family:* tofu (made of soybeans), green beans, lentils, and split peas, as well as regular beans, like kidney beans, lima beans, black beans, etc. These plant products are good sources of protein when combined with a grain product—e.g., a bowl of pea soup and a slice of whole wheat bread. Many cultures around the world have long ago discovered this healthful combination: rice-and-beans in Latin America; tofu (soybeans)-and-rice in Asia; succotash (corn-and-beans) from American Indians; falafel (chickpeas and pita bread) in the Middle East.

4. *Cut way, way down on sugar* (you probably can't eliminate it 100 percent). Read food labels. Corn syrup, sucrose, dextrose,* etc., are only different names for sugar. Products marked "no fat" usually contain lots more sugar than they ordinarily would.

5. *Spread out your eating so you have four or five mini-meals a day instead of three large ones.* Don't go for more than four hours without eating something. (When you go somewhere, take along some food—good food may not be readily available).

6. *Avoid caffeine.* Gradually wean yourself off coffee (even decaf has *some* caffeine in it). Dr. Thomas Udhe, a for-

*Honey is a simple sugar, too, but it doesn't seem to elicit the insulin reaction the way sugar does. For this reason, it's acceptable in small amounts (in bread, for example).

mer researcher at the National Institute of Mental Health, says: "Caffeine can cause panic attacks in panic-disorder patients and, in sufficient quantities, can also trigger panic attacks in normal controls."

7. *Drink six to eight glasses of water a day* (you may include some fruit juice, too). Water is the body's most important nutrient!

8. *Go easy on fats.* That means, go easy on meat and poultry, too. Even if you trim off the visible fat, you can't get rid of it all—it's in the tissue itself. Use olive oil and/or canola oil for cooking (put on low heat). Switch to fat-free milk. You can get used to the taste gradually by mixing in ever-increasing amounts with your regular milk. Avoid products that contain "partially hydrogenated oils." The process of hydrogenation produces trans-fatty acids, which scientists believe are harmful to the arteries.

9. *Go easy on salt.* Restaurant food, canned goods, processed meat, hard cheese—all these are very high in salt. Check your natural foods stores for better-but-similar products. Use more herbs and spices for flavoring.

10. *Eat a varied diet.* Don't keep eating the same foods all the time. Try new vegetables, new fruits; sample new breads and grains (rice, millet, buckwheat, etc.).

The Food Pyramids

Nutritionists tell us that the diet should consist mainly of *complex carbohydrates.* What are they? Fruits and vegetables plus whole grains.

We're all familiar with the Food Pyramid put out by the U.S. Department of Agriculture, where grains occupy the base of the pyramid (the area where most of your daily food intake should come from). However, we think there's a far better food model to follow: the California Cuisine Pyramid, formulated by the UCLA Center for Human Nutrition.* This eating guide places *fruits and vegetables* at the base of the Pyramid, with whole grains just above it. The next tier up are the protein foods: Beans, tofu, nonfat milk, seafood, poultry, egg whites, and lean meats. These foods are to be eaten in smaller amounts. At the apex of the Pyramid are the Flavor Enhancers: They give your food a good taste and are to be used sparingly: Olive oil, canola oil, nuts, avocados, spices, herbs, olives, seeds, cheese, chili peppers, and garlic.

This eating plan is not only sound nutrition, it's also helping thousands control their food carvings and attain normal weight. So if you're overweight, there is an extra bonus for you!

A Quick Evaluation

To evaluate your present diet, try this. On a piece of paper draw several of these diagrams:

Protein (animal sources)	Fruits, Veg., Beans
Miscellaneous	Whole Grains

For the next three days, keep track of everything you eat by putting a line in the appropriate box. At the end of the day, count the lines. If you've been eating the way you should, you'll have more lines on the *right* side of the diagram. For example:

Protein (animal sources) I I I	Fruits, Veg., Beans 卌
Miscellaneous I I I	Whole Grains 卌 I

*To learn more about the California Cuisine Pyramid, read *The Resolution Diet,* by David Heber, M.D. (Avery Publishing Group, 1999).

Think Before You Eat

You've just finished a delicious meal. You put your napkin to your lips and murmur a few words of appreciation to the cook. As far as you're concerned, the meal is over.

But is it? As far as your body is concerned, the meal has just begun. Your body must now extract all the nutrients it needs to serve you better. Are you a good provider? Are you supplying the necessary raw materials?

We don't want you to feel that you must never, ever—under penalty of immediate panic attack—let even a small piece of chocolate or a smidgen of cake cross your lips. After all, in our society, good times and eating go together. We want you to live a good, normal life—which means going to parties, visiting friends, traveling, and so on. We know how tempting it is to see others eating all these forbidden foods. If you give in once in a while, the sky won't fall down. When your health returns and you're no longer in a run-down condition, an *occasional* taste (we don't mean binge) isn't going to harm you.

Altogether banishing such foods from your life ("I'll never, ever eat another piece of cake again as long as I live!") may only intensify your craving for them.

If you *do* have something sweet occasionally, have it *with* something, preferably a protein food. The impact of sugar or coffee is greater on an empty stomach, and the blood sugar level rises much too quickly.

So please be easy on yourself and use common sense. An occasional looking-the-other-way is simply allowing yourself to be human. Just realize that your job is to feed and nourish *all* your body cells—not just your taste buds.

If you want to learn more about nutrition and new food products, an excellent and reliable source of information is *Nutrition Action,* a colorful magazine put out by the Center for Science in the Public Interest (CSPI), a nonprofit organization. Do consider subscribing to it; their address is: 1875 Connecticut Ave., N.W., Suite #300, Washington, D.C. 20009.

Food for Thought

• *Fruits and Vegetables:* Food shopping used to be a lot simpler; but today many new chemicals are added to our food. Some of these chemicals have not been properly tested. Some have and are still on the market despite unfavorable reports. So try to buy organically grown fruits and vegetables that have not been sprayed with harmful insecticides. If you live in a part of the country where such foods aren't available, an alternative is to grow your own. There are many helpful books available on home gardening.

• *Bread:* In many areas of the country, whole wheat bread is now standard fare at the supermarket. (The package should say "whole wheat" not just "wheat.") If at all possible, buy your breads at the natural food store or local bakery. Such breads usually lack the chemical additives of commercial bread, and they're generally made without hydrogenated shortening.

• *Beans:* Legumes (members of the bean family) have long been neglected in the typical American diet. They're an excellent source of complex carbohydrates. They have consistently been shown to cause a slow rather than a steep rise in blood sugar level. (Some researchers believe that's due to their high fiber content.)

If you've been avoiding beans because of gas discomfort, here's what you can do: Put the beans in water (a one to five ratio of beans to water) and boil for ten minutes. Let the beans soak in this water overnight. Then drain this water and continue the recipe with fresh water. Some of the vitamins will be lost this way, but the protein will still be available. Or you can use Beano (a product you buy at the drugstore); it has an enzyme that helps you digest the beans.

• *Fruit Juice:* Whenever possible, eat the raw fruit rather than drinking the juice. Fruit contains fructose (a simple sugar), but it also contains fiber and pulp, which the body breaks down slowly. Fruit juice, on the other hand, belongs more in the category of a refined food, since the fiber and pulp have been removed. If you're having juice, limit your serving to four ounces.

• *Milk:* You may wonder if you can safely drink milk because of the connection between lactic acid and panic attacks. Don't worry. The lactose found in milk is processed in the digestive tract and has nothing to do with the lactic acid our own bodies make. So unless you happen to be allergic to milk, go ahead and drink it.

• *Meat:* Meat contains a high percentage of fat. Besides, hormones and antibiotics are often injected into cattle for greater growth. For these and other reasons, many doctors are now recommending that their patients cut down on the consumption of red meat. If you do eat beef, pork, or chicken, keep the portions small and add lots of vegetables—not the other way around.

• *Artificial Sweeteners:* We don't recommend them. The long-term effects of these products are still unknown. Besides, you can retrain your taste buds to need less sweetening. How? By stopping all excess sugar for a month. Try it and see. You'll find that your present sugary foods are simply too sweet for your taste.

• *Food Irradiation:* We're wary of this new food-preservation method. It involves zapping the food with high-energy, ionizing radiation. Not only are some nutrients lost in some cases, but certain by-products of the radiation process itself have been found in the food. Although these by-products appear in very small quantities, they are unique to the radiation process and therefore of great concern to many scientists.

Vitamins

Should you or shouldn't you be taking vitamins? We strongly suggest that you do. But with this caution: Vitamins are *not* food substitutes. They are only food *supplements*.

Good nutrition must come from the diet, not from pills. You can't just eat anything you want to, and then take some pills to "make up for it." It doesn't work that way.

So why should you be taking vitamins? Your body has been exhausted and depleted because of the stress you've undergone, both the original stress that brought on the panic attacks in the first place and the daily stress you've been going through as a result of the repeated attacks. And you'll soon be going to new places or places you haven't been to in a long time. So you need all the help you can get.

The B-vitamins, long known to be essential for proper nerve function, are particularly deficient in the typical American diet, because they have been milled out of the flour. (In white enriched bread, almost two dozen nutrients have been removed, but only four put back.)

Some of the B-vitamins—B-1 (thiamine), B-3 (niacinamide), and B-6 (pyrodoxine)—are especially important in helping the body get rid of lactic acid. This is very significant, in view of what we said earlier about lactic acid and its relation to panic attacks. But these vitamins should not be taken by themselves, since they work best when taken with other members of the B-complex. And, in turn, the "B's" work together with other vitamins.

A number of clients have asked me (SS) which brand of vitamins I take. I happen to like the vitamin/mineral/antioxidant combination formulated by Kenneth Cooper, M.D., and his colleagues. Dr. Cooper (who coined the term "aerobics") is one of the foremost researchers in physical fitness and preventive medicine. I trust his judgment. (If you'd like more information about his vitamin formula, call toll-free 1-888-393-2221.)

The only important nutrient this vitamin complex doesn't supply is calcium. We need at least 1,200 milligrams of calcium a day—and most of it should come from food. Two 8-ounce glasses of skim milk provide you with 800 milligrams of calcium. An ounce of hard cheese, or one or two slices, gives you about 200 milligrams; a cup of plain yogurt, 400 milligrams; a 4-ounce serving of orange juice fortified with calcium, 200 milligrams. Two green vegetables—such as 1/2 cup of kale and 1/2 cup of broccoli—provide about 330 milligrams (although be aware that the calcium in vegetables is not as available to the body as the calcium found in dairy products). If you total that up, you have enough calcium to meet your daily requirement.

If, for any reason, you can't have dairy products—or if your daily intake of calcium is less than the recommended amount—you should consider taking calcium supplements. Calcium citrate (as in Citracal) would be an excellent choice, according to Dr. Cooper, because this form of calcium is more readily absorbed by the body.

K-Rations for Courage

When you first start going back to those places you now fear, your emotions will be like those of a soldier going to the front lines. You will wonder: Will I come out of the "battle" okay? Will I make it? The high adrenaline output that can accompany such thoughts can be very draining.

Worry uses up a lot of energy. It can therefore rapidly deplete the normal supply of sugar in the blood. For that reason it's prudent to eat before you go and/or to carry with you an emergency "K-ration."

There are certain foods that will cause a relatively slow, steady rise in blood sugar level and help sustain your energy. Such foods are said to be low on the "glycemic index," a scale that measures the degree to which the food triggers blood sugar and insulin responses. Therefore, select your K-rations from the following list: apples, pears, oranges, grapefruit, cantaloupe, sweet potato, green peas, chickpeas, lentil soup, spaghetti, All-Bran cereal, skim milk, lowfat yogurt. (You can have other foods too, but these are best.)

Breakfast—A Very Important Meal

You've heard it many times before: Breakfast is a very important meal. It gives you a boost in energy and gets the brain and body going. If you get up in the morning and can't even look at food, chances are you had too much for dinner last night; you went down for a midnight snack; or you have the radio or TV news on.

Even if you're very rushed in the morning, breakfast is a cinch to make, especially with the products available today. After all, how long does it take to boil water? You can have a hot, nourishing cereal with the prepackaged envelopes that you just tear open, pour into a bowl, and add boiling water. How long does it take to pour yourself a cup of orange juice? Or to make a hard-boiled egg the night before?

If you prefer dry cereal with cold milk and fruit on top, that's OK, too. There are some very good cereals on the market—and some very bad ones. Ask the store clerk where the "healthy cereals" are kept (sometimes they're on another shelf, in a corner . . .). Check the list of ingredients—the fine print, not what it says on the front of the package. It'll be an eye-opener for you.

I mention cereals and juice for breakfast simply because they're the easiest to prepare. But, really, you can have just about anything for breakfast—why not? I've had "suppers" for breakfast—sandwiches, stews, soup.

Be adventurous. Try something new.

Three Principles for Easy Meal Preparation

If, like many people, you don't have the time or inclination to prepare elaborate meals, don't despair; you can still eat healthily. I (SS) want to show you how easy it is to prepare tasty, nutritious meals with a minimum of effort. There are three basic principles to follow.

The first principle is to shop wisely. Buy the important foods, the good foods, based on the Food Pyramid.

When I go to the supermarket, the first place I visit is the produce section. I buy a variety of items—whatever looks fresh and inviting. After loading my cart with fruits and vegetables, I shop for grains and dairy products. I don't bring home any junk food because I don't want to be tempted. Besides, there are so many delicious snacks I can fix for myself that are part of a good diet, who needs junk food?

The second principle is to cook ahead. Do it in stages—and stockpile your food.

A lot of people cook only enough food for one day. Anything they don't eat they call "leftovers." But who wants to eat something called "leftovers"? When I cook, I purposely make a lot more than I can use at one time. Who wants to cook every day? Who has time? Food can keep (at least for a while). We have refrigerators, we have freezers. What's the point of having these conveniences if we're not going to use them?

I also suggest you prepare your food in stages. Who says you have to do it all at once? For example, the other night while waiting for my TV show to come on, I peeled and cut up some vegetables for something I planned to make the next day. You don't have to spend a solid hour in the kitchen—unless, of course, you want to. You can spend five minutes here, ten minutes there; it all adds up.

Do you ever watch cooking shows on TV? Have you noticed how the chef lays out all the ingredients in front of him, some already cut, some even precooked? All he does is take something from this dish, something from that dish, mix them together, throw them in the fry pan . . . and voila! Well, you can do the same thing!

You've probably heard the dictum that if you can break up an onerous task into small, manageable pieces, it ceases to be overwhelming. The same applies to cooking. If you want to make a dish and you already have some of the ingredients on hand cooked or partly cooked, your job becomes much easier.

I'll give you an example. The other day, while I was in the kitchen doing some other cooking, I fried an onion with mushrooms. Simple, right? I just sprayed the pan with olive oil spray, put in the two ingredients, and let them sauté a little bit. Then I added just a little bit of water (about 1/2 cup), covered the pan, and let the vegetables stew. When they were tender, I let them cool, then put them away in the fridge in a little container.

The next day, I took some broccoli out of the fridge and cut off a few florets. I opened a can of pinto beans, drained them, and put these two ingredients in a bowl. (Not hard to do, right?) I squirted a little bit of lemon juice on these, then added the fried onions and mushrooms I had made the day before. I shook in some spices (celery seed and dill), mixed everything together—and it was delicious! If I'd had cooked noodles on hand, I probably would have thrown them in, too.

You can vary this dish in a hundred different ways: Use a different kind of beans, different vegetables, a different kind of pasta—the variations are endless.

And you can have a meal on the table in literally minutes.

Not long ago, I met my friend Lisa at the library. We decided to go to a particular place that afternoon, and we had to be there by a certain time. I invited Lisa to come to my house for lunch first; then I glanced at my watch and realized we barely had time to eat.

"Don't worry," I told her, "I can have lunch on the table in five minutes."

She told me she'd hold me to it—and time me. So we made a bet. And guess what? I won! (In fact, lunch was ready in four minutes, not five.)

So that's the advantage of having a well-stocked fridge. You have ready dishes to choose from. And when hunger strikes and you want something "right away"—there it is! You won't reach for the instant "junk" food and say afterward, "Oops, I did it again!" If you stock the right foods, anything you grab will give you good nutrition.

Now, you may think it's just easier and less messy to cook everything at once (and get it over with)—especially when you're putting together a dish of many ingredients. Well . . . maybe—*if* you're only cooking it that one time. But if you have to prepare meals day after day, week after week, cooking ahead and doing it piecemeal (when you have time and you feel like it) works best. You're not under pressure ("I must get this done by five o'clock!") and you can enjoy your time in the kitchen.

The third principle that makes meal preparation easier and faster is to incorporate ready-made (store-bought) products into your recipes wherever possible.

Everyone is so busy these days—and the food manufacturers know this. That's why there are so many convenience foods on the market.

But (and this "but" is important!) the trouble with most of these products is that they're too high in salt (unless they specifically state on the label "no salt added"); they have too many chemical additives and hydrogenated oil; and they're often high in fat (unless marked "nonfat"). Even foods marked "low-fat" may not necessarily be so. So it's very important to read the labels. Not on the front of the package (where the manufacturer can say just about anything he wants) but on the back or side where it says "List of Ingredients." There, the manufacturer is mandated by the FDA to tell the truth. Only use a ready-made product if it meets your nutritional standards.

With these three principles in mind (bringing the right foods home . . . preparing them in small, easy steps and stockpiling them . . . and supplementing them with "health-friendly" store-bought foods), cooking *really* becomes interesting. And creative.

"But I Hate That Food!"

Many people say, "I hate peas." Or broccoli. Or carrots. For years I (SS) used to say, "I like all foods—except pea soup." I was thinking of my mother's thick pea-soup potage. (Yech!) Then one day, a friend served a wonderful soup.

"This is *so* delicious," I said. "What is it?"

"Pea soup," my friend said.

Oh.

Kale is another vegetable most people don't like. Yet in all the nutrition charts I've seen, kale is always high up on the list of excellent foods. For a long time, I looked for a good recipe for kale—and couldn't find any. But when I tried mixing it in with noodles, fried onions, and tomato sauce (or in soup), I found it was delicious!

See? It all depends on how you prepare the food; how you season it; how you combine it with other foods, etc.

So, if you always thought you hated a particular (nutritious) food and never went near it, give it a chance. Experiment. You never know till you try . . . !

And "trying" is so much easier when you have things ready and on hand: steamed veggies, canned goods, etc. By following the three principles and dreaming up new combinations, you can create an astronomical number of easy, healthy dishes!

Prototype Recipes

A prototype recipe is one that can be used as the basis for many different dishes simply by varying a few of the ingredients. Here are a few examples:

Fruit or Vegetable "Pie"

~

1. Cut (and peel if you desire) fruit or vegetables into small chunks. Put about 4 cups worth into a large bowl. If you're working with a vegetable like broccoli or cauliflower, steam it first. If you're preparing carrots or zucchini, you may prefer to shred or grate them.

2. Dip 4 slices of whole wheat bread into a dish of liquid and squeeze out the excess. The liquid can be water or juice—anything that seems to go with the fruit or vegetable you're preparing. Crumble up the bread with your fingers and add it to the bowl of fruit or vegetables.

3. Throw in a handful of raisins and, if you like, seasonings of your choice.

4. Add 1 or 2 beaten egg whites.

5. Mix everything together and pour the mixture into a baking dish greased with olive or canola oil. Bake at 325° until it "looks done"—about an hour.

NOTE: Here are some of the combinations I have tried (they are all great!):

apples, with grapefruit juice

assortment of fruit, with grape juice

cauliflower, with water (I sprinkled some sugar on top when it was done)

carrots, with orange juice

broccoli, with tomato juice

zucchini, with pineapple juice

Baked Vegetables

~

My friend Marie-Jean La Croix suggested this recipe.

1. *In a casserole dish that has a cover, put one or two packages of frozen mixed vegetables (depending on the size of your casserole dish) or use 2 or 3 cups bite-sized pieces of mixed fresh vegetables, putting the "harder" vegetables on the bottom.*

2. *Slice a raw onion and place the slices on top of the vegetables. As the onion bakes, it "melts," dripping down moisture and flavor.*

3. *Pour 1/2 cup water or tomato juice over the vegetables. If desired, add seasoning: salt and pepper, "Italian spices," "Chinese spices," etc.*

4. *Cover and bake at 350° for about an hour. (If you like your vegetables firmer, remove the dish ten minutes or so earlier.)*

NOTE: If you want to add meat-protein to this dish, use thawed or precooked boneless chicken breast. Just put it on the bottom of the casserole dish. Baking time would be about an hour if chicken was raw and 30 minutes if chicken was precooked. (Make sure the chicken is well-done; it should *not* be pink inside.)

Salad

~

Some people think a salad has to contain only vegetables like lettuce, tomatoes, and cucumbers. It doesn't. You can add fruit, too: apples, oranges, kiwi, pears, grapes, avocado, although not necessarily all at the same time. Or use interesting heartier vegetables such as broccoli florets or grated carrot. I never use iceberg lettuce; it has very little nutritional value. Instead, use Romaine or red-leaf lettuce. I often make a dressing of olive oil, lemon juice, and a touch of garlic powder, with a sprinkling of salad herbs.

Here are some more good salad combinations:

Spinach Salad: Fresh spinach, mushrooms, and onion rings.

Red, Green, and Orange Salad: Deep green lettuce, orange segments, and sweet red pepper.

Potato Salad: Cook cut-up potatoes and allow them to cool. In a separate bowl, mix equal amounts of nonfat lemon yogurt with light sour cream. Fold the potatoes gently into this mixture. Add scallions, chopped red and/or green pepper, peas, etc.

Hearty Tuna Salad: Add a can of tuna or salmon (drained and flaked) to your fruit and vegetable salads. (No need to add mayo—just use salad dressing.)

Vegetable Soup

~

What could be more inviting on a cold winter day than a bowl of hot soup? The easy way to make a nutritionally enriched soup is to use a commercial soup as your base, then add: anything from the bean family; cooked or steamed carrots; yams; some of the more nutritious-but-not-so-popular vegetables such as kale or collard greens. One of the most delicious soups I ever tasted was seasoned with canned turnip greens.

Some excellent commercial soups are the Tabatchnick line of frozen soups and Health Valley Fat-Free Chicken Broth Soup. Be aware that commercial soups are usually very high in salt (over 500 milligrams sodium per serving). You can get around that problem by diluting the soup or by cutting down on salt elsewhere in your diet.

Cinnamon-Walnut "Coffee Cake"

~

When I (SS) worked in an office, the coffee wagon would come around every morning loaded with all sorts of baked goods. My favorite was a crunchy coffee cake. When I decided to eat in a more health-conscious way, I wondered what I could substitute for my beloved coffee cake. What exactly did I like about that particular cake? Well . . . I liked the crunchiness—the walnuts and raisins—and the taste of cinnamon. And that's how I came up with this recipe:

Toast 2 slices of whole wheat bread. Spread cottage cheese or fresh farmer cheese on the toast. Dot with raisins and chopped walnuts and sprinkle with cinnamon and sugar (mixed, in a shaker). Who says you can't have your cake and eat it too?

Further Food for Thought

Caffeine and Panic Attacks

I (SS) remember one of the first clients I had at PASS. He was a young surgical resident who was having a problem with panic attacks. He was often unable to operate because his hands were shaking so much. When I inquired about his diet, he mentioned that he had about twenty cups of coffee a day! I told him that was one of the reasons he was having panic attacks. His indignant reply was, "That can't be right. I've been drinking lots of coffee for years and it never bothered me before!" (He didn't stop to consider that he was evidently under much greater stress now.) "Besides," he went on, "there's nothing in the medical literature that says there's any connection between coffee and panic attacks."

Well, there certainly is now. Dr. Thomas Udhe, a former researcher at the National Institute of Mental Health, did a study that demonstrated the detrimental effects of caffeine on panic-prone individuals. He has called caffeine the world's most widely used mood-altering drug.

Caffeine is found not only in coffee, but also in tea, soft drinks, and chocolate! It's also usually found in certain over-the-counter headache or cold remedies.

If you're in the habit now of taking large amounts of caffeine daily, you can help prevent withdrawal symptoms by tapering off *gradually*.

Alcohol and Panic Attacks

Sometimes a person will say, "I'm nervous, I need a drink." Often a person won't admit his dependence on alcohol, yet heads for the bar just the same. But alcohol, like a high-sugar diet, does not solve the problem; in fact, it only makes it worse. It offers a quick fix, but there's hell to pay later.

The liver, in addition to being a storehouse for sugar, also has the ability to manufacture sugar from scratch (it uses the body's protein and fat to do this). This is done on an emergency basis after the body's own reserves of sugar have been used up. But alcohol blocks the liver's ability to do this. That means that if alcohol is taken on an empty stomach, without other food, the blood sugar level can drop dangerously low. And there's another factor, too: A too-high intake of alcohol depletes the body of certain nutrients—just as a high-sugar diet does.

We think many problem drinkers are really panic attack sufferers who are attempting to steady their nerves with alcohol. The catch is that it doesn't work.

Cigarettes and Panic Attacks

If you're a smoker, you've no doubt been equating cigarettes with relaxation. But scientific findings prove otherwise: Nicotine stimulates the sympathetic nervous system, and that's exactly what you don't want. The reason you feel better immediately after you inhale is because you've raised your blood sugar level. But don't forget, there's a rebound reaction later, just as there is with sugar.

A Swedish study (reported in the British medical journal *Lancet*) showed a sharp rise in blood sugar level—as high as 35 percent—while smoking. The rapid fall that occurred later, said one researcher, "throws further light on the habit of chain-smoking . . . and the craving for another pick-me-up." When smokers were given cigarettes without the nicotine, the sharp rise and subsequent fall didn't occur.

You know, of course, without our telling you, how smoking cuts your oxygen intake.

Only Part of the Picture

Paying attention to your diet is essential to your recovery, but remember, diet is only one facet of the recovery program. It is not the total picture. If you harbor all sorts of negative beliefs and see danger in every corner, you'll still have a problem with panic attacks. This constant stress and anxiety will soon wear out your alarm system. You have to change other aspects of your life as well, by working on the other six steps of the program.

CHAPTER 6

Step 2: Relaxation

"Anything you do over and over again, you get better at. It's just a law of Nature."
—*Jack Canfield*

At a phobia conference, we once saw a videotape of a young woman who had previously been homebound. The film showed her going on a bus trip for the first time. Throughout the entire trip, the young woman sat with clenched fists, then wringing her hands over and over again. The cameraman then kept zooming in on her hands. Had this young woman on the bus been taught to relax her voluntary muscles before and during the trip, she would have been able to enjoy the bus trip a little more, instead of sitting there in absolute agony.

Relaxation is the antithesis of anxiety. Relaxation and anxiety cannot co-exist. If you're generally a very anxious person, what you have to do is pull back and start moving toward the opposite extreme. Not that you'll ever reach that extreme, but the fact that you're *moving* in that direction will eventually let you wind up somewhere in the middle. In other words, normal. (Which is what you want, right?)

Now, relaxation comes in different sizes, so to speak— anywhere from a momentary relaxed feeling (letting go; feeling the downward pull of gravity; making your body feel "heavy," etc.) to an extended period of relaxation, that deeply relaxed feeling you might get as you lie down, eyes closed, listening to a relaxation tape.

Both types of relaxation—the momentary and the prolonged—are very important and necessary. The momentary relaxation helps you cope while you're actually *in* the feared situation, and the extended relaxation that you practice daily makes it easier for you to momentarily relax. You need *both* kinds of relaxation.

Relaxation is a skill. And, like any other skill, it can be learned. But it needs constant, daily practice. Your muscles somehow learn what relaxation feels like—by doing. They just get into a relaxed state more easily. It's like learning to dance: Somehow, after practicing many times, you just get out on the dance floor—and you do it. It just comes to you without thinking much about it.

As part of the recovery program we recommend that you practice relaxation every day. What will daily relaxation practice do for you? It will tone down your general state of nervousness and reduce the irritability of the nervous system. Little things won't bother you as much. You won't be so over-anxious all the time.

As we said earlier, it is physically impossible to be anxious (or to have a panic attack) and be relaxed at the same time. A muscle fiber is either all stretched out or tightly coiled. There's no in-between. It's like a light: It's either on or off. Muscle fibers work together in groups. As more and more muscle groups let go and uncoil, the tendency is for other muscle groups to join them—and the relaxation deepens. So by relaxing as many *voluntary* muscles as you can reach, you're relaxing the corresponding nerve cells, too. That's the whole idea: to get as many nerve cells as you can involved in the relaxation process *before* tension builds up.

There are two sets of nerves that connect the brain and the muscles. One set of nerves (sensory nerves) bring in sensations and information *from* the environment; another set of nerves (motor nerves) bring our messages *to* the environment. We touch, we move, we listen. Both sets of nerves are constantly being activated because we are always interacting with our environment. When one is deeply relaxed, nerve messages are dampened down. They're quieted. They rest. Thus, the relaxation period becomes a welcome respite to an overworked nervous system.

Occasionally a client will report having difficulty with the idea of relaxing. It turns out that what they really fear is letting go. Because this is often equated with "losing control," and that's a scary thought to most panic attack sufferers.

May we suggest that you substitute the words, "getting floppy." It's a friendlier, even a more accurate, way of describing it. (This suggestion was given to us by Maralyn L. Teare, formerly a clinical instructor of psychiatry at a medical center in Los Angeles.)

Techniques for Relaxation

There are many different ways to teach your muscles to relax. Here are some that we have found helpful. The shorter methods, which bring momentary relaxation, can be put to use in actual panic situations to help relieve tension. Learn to do these techniques and use them as relaxation tools whenever you need them. The final method, prolonged relaxation, produces a different, healing type of relaxation known as deep relaxation, and should be practiced every day.

Abdominal Breathing ("Belly Puffs")

Did you know that when you take shallow breaths from the upper chest, you are activating the sympathetic nervous system? And that when you're under stress (i.e., when the sympathetic nervous system is already activated) your body switches *automatically* to upper chest breathing? They go hand in hand. Many nervous people are unaware that they're breathing from the upper chest and taking shallow breaths. If you breathe this way, you pave the way for hyper-ventilation because you're often not getting enough air and your body tries to compensate by breathing more.

On the other hand, abdominal breathing (or diaphrag-matic breathing, as it's sometimes called) is associated with the parasympathetic nervous system, the calming one. It also brings in more oxygen to the lower lobes of the lungs—about 25 percent more, which can make a significant differ-ence in the way you feel.

Fortunately, our breathing is partly under voluntary con-trol. That means you can switch at will to diaphragmatic breathing whenever you're under stress.

Here's how you do it:

1. Sit up straight. Inhale deeply and slowly through your nose. As you inhale, your belly should push out a bit. (If you're having trouble doing it, make believe you're try-ing to blow up a balloon in your belly.) Hold for a count of 4.
2. Purse your lips and exhale slowly through your mouth. As you exhale (this is important), you'll notice a (slight) relaxed feeling going down your thighs, knees, legs. *Concentrate on that feeling.*

I think of abdominal breathing as "belly puffs" because you just do it now and then (*not* continuously) just as you would puff on a cigarette (heaven forbid!).

So whenever you're in a sitting position, feeling tense, take a few "belly puffs"—and relax.

The Six-Second Relaxation Break

The QR

The QR is a powerful tool for ridding yourself of tension. QR stands for Quieting Reflex. It's a technique that was devel-

oped by Charles F. Stroebel, M.D., a Connecticut-based neu-
rologist/psychiatrist. The QR is simple to do—it takes only six
seconds, but it is remarkably effective in relieving tension.*

1. *Stop or s-l-o-w down* (sit, if you wish).
2. *Relax your facial muscles* by doing the following:
   a. Smile inwardly.
   b. Imagine the smile coming across your face and
      spreading up towards your eyes. (Make sure your
      teeth and jaw are unclenched.)
   c. Say to yourself: "My eyes are twinkling and sparkling."
3. *Take a deep abdominal breath.*
   a. Imagine you are inhaling through holes in the bot-
      toms of your feet, up through your legs, and into
      your stomach.
   b. Feel the upward flow of warmth and "heaviness."
4. *As you exhale slowly:*
   a. Imagine the air flowing back down through holes in
      your feet, taking all the tension along with it.
   b. At the same time, let your jaw, tongue, and shoul-
      ders go limp.

(Repeat once more.)

You're probably wondering: How can such a simple technique be so helpful? Here's the rationale behind it.

1. The hypothalamus, the body's sentry, is constantly
receiving messages of the state of tension (or relaxation) of
all the muscles in the body. (This is without our conscious
awareness.) If the sentry receives messages that the muscles
are generally in a relaxed state, the sentry relaxes too. Therefore, when you slow down (and don't rush), you're encouraging your over-alert sentry to relax too.

*Reprinted by permission. *QR: The Quieting Reflex* by Charles F. Stroebel, M.D.,
Berkley Publishing, 1983.

2. Notice that this exercise involves many muscles in the facial area. Remember, muscles and nerves are connected. The corresponding nerve cells of the facial muscles occupy a large part of the brain. For example, there are more nerve bundles for your tongue than, say, for a much larger area in your back. Therefore, what the facial muscles do carries a lot of weight, so to speak. When the facial muscles relax, a great number of nerve bundles in the brain relax too.

As you will soon see, you can help your body relax through the use of appropriate imagery. The cells can't tell the difference between what's real and what isn't. If you imagine relief in the form of warmth and comfort, your muscle cells respond and let go.

The jaws are generally clenched during stress; the shoulder muscles are tight and hunched up (ready for fight or flight). Therefore, if you relax those muscles consciously, it conveys this message to the sentry and helps counteract any stress buildup.

3. The deep breathing helps provide more oxygen to the brain, and it also helps to relax the chest muscles.

4. Powerful imagery is evoked when you "see" all the tension leaving your body (what a relief *that* is!).

So, whenever you begin to feel tense or hurried, that should be a signal for you to immediately switch gears and do the QR. You can do it 100, 200 times a day; the more you practice, the better, because it will reinforce the QR as a response to tension, and after a while the response will become automatic.

Do you see what a valuable tool this can be? You can do the QR anywhere, in almost any situation. And all it takes is a moment of your time. (Even if you do it 100 times, it's still only ten minutes a day.)

A "Calming Stone"

About a year ago, I (SS) was invited to go on a spiritual retreat. It was summertime and the retreat took place in a lovely garden. At the end of the day, as we all sat in a circle, the leader said a prayer and blessed us. Then she passed around a dish of small stones. We were each to take one stone and hold it in our hand. I chose a smooth pink one. Next, we each sent a blessing to someone in the group, naming that person. It was such a nice—and, yes, spiritual—moment.

After I got home, I put my stone on the kitchen window sill. Often, I'd take the stone in my hand and look out the window at Nature—the trees, the birds—and I'd think of how peaceful I felt at that spiritual retreat. After doing this a number of times, I found that just holding the stone, feeling it in my hand, would bring me instant relaxation and peace. That's why I call it my "calming stone."

What I did, you see, is train my autonomic nervous system to respond with relaxation to a certain stimulus (like Pavlov did with his dogs).

You can do something similar. Just find a suitable small object—or buy one. Or paste a picture or photograph or "lucky penny" on a small piece of cardboard. The important thing is that you associate that object with a peaceful or pleasant emotion. Invent a ceremony that will make this object even more meaningful to you. And always, as you hold the object in your hand, think beautiful thoughts. Just for those few seconds. Do it many times. And pretty soon, those two thoughts in your mind—the peace, the object—will intertwine, and you'll have found your own "calming stone."

The Two-Minute Relaxation Break

Eye Relaxation Exercises

Did you know that the eyes are considered an extension of the brain? And that if the eyes are completely relaxed, it's easier for the whole body to become relaxed too?

Here are some eye exercises that you can do from time to time during the day. One advantage of these exercises is that you can do them almost anywhere, even at work.

Palming: Place your elbows on a table. Cup both hands and put them over your eyes so that your face rests in the palms of your hands. Don't touch your eyes at all; merely hold the bony structure around your eyes. Sit this way for a few moments, thinking of pleasant scenes of nature or places you'd like to visit.

Eye-Writing: You can sit or lie down. Close your eyes. Simply "draw" some figure 8's, circles, letters of the alphabet, etc., by moving your eyes.

Near Vision/Far Vision: Whenever you read a lot or do close work, rest your eyes from time to time by looking for a few moments at distant objects. This is especially important if you work with a computer.

The Five-Minute Relaxation Break

Slow, "Soft" Stretches

If you're more tense than usual before you begin the deep-relaxation session, or if you want to achieve a greater degree of relaxation, take five or ten minutes to prepare yourself with slow, physical movement.

Soft stretches stretch out the muscles and gently ease away tension. Dr. Edmund Jacobson, a Chicago physician who began his research in relaxation techniques back in the 1920s, noted that when you tense a muscle, hold the tension for some seconds, and then let go, the subsequent relaxation of the muscle is greater than if you hadn't tensed the muscle at all.

The effect is very much akin to that of stylized Chinese exercise, tai chi chuan, done every morning in Chinese town squares by young and old alike. Because when you do the exercises very slowly, you are holding the tension for several seconds.

You can simply turn on the radio, find some soft music, and dance freestyle. Do a variety of body movements very, very slowly, holding the pose for as long as you comfortably can.

The Half-Hour Relaxation Break—Prolonged Relaxation

Many people say they relax while watching TV or knitting. But this is not the relaxation we mean. We mean *deep* relaxation, where, for a period of twenty to thirty minutes a day, your body is so relaxed that it becomes as limp and loose as a rag doll.

Deep-relaxation sessions not only relieve momentary tension and anxiety, their effects are cumulative, carrying over into real-life situations as well. Each time you practice relaxation, you are training your muscles to know what complete relaxation feels like. So you're making it easier for them to remember the relaxed state. Thus, you can help head off a panic attack *before* it starts. You relax *before* the tension builds up—and overwhelms you.

So it's important that you set aside a definite time period of between twenty and thirty minutes every day to practice deep-relaxation exercises. Lock the door, take the phone off the hook, have your husband watch the children for half an hour. Do whatever you have to do to ensure privacy, peace, and quiet. This is *your* block of time—for getting well!

Some people feel guilty when they take time for themselves. They see it as time taken away from their family. If this is how you feel, think of this: If you're sick, how can you take care of others? The best gift you can give your family is to be your best self. And this means you have to make the time to take care of your health—both your mental and your physical health.

Probably the most important prerequisite for a good relaxation session is a passive, nonresistant attitude. This doesn't mean we want you to become a passive person. But during this half hour or so, we recommend that you let down your guard and become more receptive, more passive. Why? Because this is in the *opposite* direction of the fight-or-flight response. When the sympathetic nervous system has gained the upper hand, you need to elicit the opposite response in order to restore a balance.

During deep relaxation, the following beneficial physio-logical changes take place:

1. Your brain wave pattern subsides to the alpha state, a characteristic of the resting state.
2. Your oxygen consumption decreases.
3. The production of lactic acid drops.

Audio Meditation

The best way to practice deep relaxation, we've found, is by means of an audio-cassette tape. This embodies all the features of time-honored meditation—something to focus your attention on (a voice), a comfortable position, and so on—yet it doesn't require the initial training period that meditation does. You simply sit in a chair, or lie down, close your eyes, and listen to a soothing voice. As you listen, you create the images and scenes in your mind that the voice sug-gests. The more involved you become in this process, the better able you are to relax.

I (SS) was first introduced to audio relaxation many years ago by my dentist, Dr. Darwin Arkow, who once told me I was the most nervous patient he ever had. One day, I was in his office to have a filling, and he gave me a shot of Novocaine containing epinephrine (another name for adrenaline). I had a panic attack right there in the dental chair, and I refused to let him work on my tooth. The next time I came to the office, he tried gas. That didn't work either; I became nauseated. So he said to me, "Look, there's only one other thing I can try. It's a deep-relaxation method, but I'll need your full cooperation." At that point, I was eager to try any-thing. He talked and I listened. In a short time, I became so relaxed that when he started drilling, I felt no pain. I was absolutely amazed that the whole procedure was so comfort-able and effective—and all he did was talk to me!

After that initial experience, I came to his office just to

get relaxed—never mind the cavities! Since I was so enthusiastic, he taped a relaxation session for me to keep. We have made a relaxation tape for PASS-Group members based on my dentist's tape. To order the PASS-Group Relaxation Tape, please see the last page of this book. Or you can use one of the relaxation tapes currently on the market.

The Deep-Relaxation Experience

What does deep relaxation feel like? It's a refreshing experience. When you open your eyes and stretch, it's as if you had a good night's peaceful sleep. Your body feels rested and your mind is clear and serene.

Here is a poem, sent in by one of our clients, Rachel Hill, that describes this feeling:

Meditation/Relaxation

A mantle of peace descends
And covers my shoulders with
Soft, white wings.

The impatience, the struggles,
The tightly woven webs
Are all swept away.

A black velvet curtain falls
And stillness comes
Like the hushed moment at dawn;
A sweet, sweet quiet
Stills my limbs and tongue and eye;
The only sound is my own soft breath.

I love my world without clocks;
Each day I feel its stillness and peace,
Each day I am renewed.

Practicing Relaxation

Sometimes clients will ask: Do I have to practice *all* those relaxation techniques? Isn't it enough just to do the deep-relaxation tape?

The answer is, you need both the longer relaxation break and the mini-breaks. So pick one or two (or more) of the short-duration exercises and add them to your daily routine—they don't take long at all. Isn't it time well spent if it leads to your recovery?

Relax and Rehearse (Visualization)

A good way to learn how to handle panic attacks is to rehearse *how you're going to act* in the situation that has been giving you trouble (e.g., the supermarket, the car, the plane, etc.) ahead of time. The best time to do this is when you're in a very relaxed state and don't have outside stimuli to distract you.

So get comfortable. Put on a relaxation tape. Get yourself really relaxed—and then: In your mind's eye, see yourself *as you would like to be.*

If "driving," for example, picture yourself sitting confidently in your car, viewing everything as you travel along—the streets, the people walking, etc. You can even practice doing the QR in your daydream, just as you would in real life, to ease the tension.

This type of rehearsal, called visualization—especially when coupled with relaxation—has been shown to be very effective in enhancing performance in the real situation. It's a technique that's used a lot in the sports world to augment on-site practice sessions.

First Aid for Panic Attacks
(And That "Pre-Panic" Feeling)

Each person experiences "that pre-panic feeling" in a slightly different way, but I'm sure you recognize the early signs of a panic attack coming on. It might be those "What-if" thoughts: "What if it happens now? What will people think?" etc. Or you might start testing your reflexes to see if they're still working: "Can I still swallow? Am I able to breathe?" (When you fear, your saliva stops flowing, so you *may* have trouble swallowing; when your chest muscles are tight from fear, you *may* find it hard to breathe normally and evenly.) Or your mind may turn inward, looking for "symptoms," and you simply stop paying attention to what's going on around you.

So your goal is to learn both how to prevent a panic attack and how to deal with one if you have to. When you know you have a backup system, when you know you can do something to help yourself, you feel more assured.

Remember the scene we described earlier: the young woman taking her first bus trip who kept wringing her hands? As I watched the film, it reminded me of the way they used to depict childbirth scenes in movies about the olden days. The mother would grab and hang on to a cloth that was tied to the bedpost whenever a contraction came. Contrast this with the natural childbirth method proposed by Dr. Grantly Dick-Read of England (*Childbirth Without Fear*). It is precisely during the contraction that the mother is taught to relax and let go, in order to allow the womb to open up. Allowing the contraction to come in a wave—without resistance or interference—greatly diminishes, and in many cases even eliminates, the pain. (Pain and fear are very similar. Both involve tense muscles; naturally, the tenser the muscle, the worse the pain—or the fear.)

Similarly, it's at the moment of panic that you have to train yourself to respond by letting go, by "getting floppy."

The natural tendency is to tense up even more. But in doing that, you're actually setting yourself up for more tension.

The best advice we can give you is this: Don't run away. Yes, we know this is exactly what you feel like doing. But don't. It is not a good strategy because the immediate sense of relief you feel by running away, retreating, only reinforces the habit of avoiding. The relief, you see, is your "reward."

But it's only a brief victory. Think about the long-term effects. How will you ever be able to attend a wedding, travel, take classes, go to restaurants—if you train yourself to leave the minute you start feeling uncomfortable? Isn't it better to stay in the situation, use the tools we're giving you, and squelch the panic attack yourself?

Here's how:

1. *Slow down, stop.* (Don't run away.) Sit down, if possible. Take several (as needed) s-l-o-w and deep abdominal breaths. Inhale slowly; hold; exhale slowly.
2. *Feel your body's "heaviness."* Allow gravity to pull at you, tug at you, in a downward direction. Become completely passive.
3. *Think health!* Remind yourself that you're healthy (conjure up your doctor's face, telling you this). Stop scaring yourself!
4. Then, *allow time for that panicky feeling to pass.* When a high level of stress chemicals are already coursing through your bloodstream, it takes a few moments for them to dissipate.

Later, when it's all over, ask yourself: How did that come on? Was it more mind or body? Did I scare myself with all those what-ifs again? Have I been pushing myself too hard lately and neglecting my health? When was the last time I ate, and what did I eat?

CHAPTER 7

Step 3: Exercise

"Exercise is like taking a Valium."
—*Jane Brody,*
science editor of
The New York Times

Why is exercise so soothing?

Pam Colari, a former dancer and physical education instructor, explains why in the following interview:

PAM: Exercise actually reduces stress. You see, stress is a form of muscle tension. When you have all the stress built up in your body, it's like a wild animal who's been angered. You're ready to pounce. And what you want to do is to reduce all this muscle tension. If you exercise, it's going to be a release from all this tension that's built up in the muscles.

We have many secretaries that come into this spa, and it's really amazing that when they come in—when we get the crew that comes in right after work—like I'm afraid to talk to half of these people. They all look so mean and so angry! So I just give them a quick hello. But when they leave, it's like, you know, "Have a nice evening"—and they feel wonderful!

SHIRLEY: This is so true. I used to go to a gym on my lunch hour. My boss was a wonderful guy, really, but sometimes he'd frazzle my nerves. I used to go to a gym so I could have an exercise break, and I'd come back to the office feeling so wonderful, so relaxed. And I'd also feel so kindly toward my boss, I'd forget how he was in the morning!

PAM: Let me add this also: When people get this stiff neck in the back, when they say, "Oh, I'm so tense, I need a massage," what happens is that the muscles have just tightened up into little balls. And by working that out, you're going to feel so much better. You can get a headache from muscle tension, too, from tightening up the muscles of the neck.

SHIRLEY: Yes, that can be a pain in the neck . . . ! Tell me, what about older women? Many people believe that because they haven't exercised regularly or they exercised and stopped that maybe it's too late for them to start now.

PAM: It's never too late. The human body is an amazing organism. You can start exercising at any time. The one important thing to keep in mind is that you should start slowly if you haven't exercised in a long time. And you should have a checkup from your doctor because there may be things you should know about. If you start exercising slowly, you'll be able to build up your body to what it should be. Then you just keep it up.

SHIRLEY: Speaking about age, it's interesting that many astronauts are in their forties—some of them in the late forties. And here these people were picked just because they were in top physical shape! So when women say to me, at age forty, I can't exercise, I'm over the hill, I have to laugh.

PAM: Sure, it's true. The body can be taught how to do almost anything. It's very trainable.

I once watched on TV a sixty-eight-year-old woman who had taken up karate a few years before to relieve arthritis, and then went on to earn a black belt—the highest award in karate. She delighted the audience by breaking wooden boards with swift kicks—and she was only four-foot-eleven and weighed about a hundred pounds.

If such a miraculous turn-around was possible for this woman, why not for you?

Aerobic Exercise

Aerobic exercise trains your body to deliver oxygen more efficiently. As your body attempts to adjust to the tough demands of these exercises, your oxygen-delivery system becomes stronger.

Here are some examples of aerobic exercises:

Swimming
Walking/running/walking
Brisk walking
Running in place
Bike riding
Rowing
Dancing (if moving arms and legs)
Jogging
Jumping rope
Calisthenics (if continuous)

There are many other exercises that help strengthen and develop the outside muscles of the body—weightlifting and yoga are two examples. But these are not aerobic. They don't teach the body to process oxygen because they don't continue long enough and they don't give the heart and lungs a good enough workout.

In order for an exercise to qualify as aerobic, it must be continuous and it must be done with sufficient energy to raise the pulse rate. A stop-and-go exercise—like softball, for example—is not aerobic. Brisk walking is an excellent aerobic exercise. (We don't recommend jogging—unless you're the athletic type who really enjoys it—because it's hard on the bone structure.) With any exercise, you have to build up your tolerance gradually. The ultimate goal should be at least a half-hour of aerobic exercise, three days a week.

Research has now shown that a slower-paced walk can also give you aerobic fitness, provided that you do it for a longer period of time—say, a full hour, three times a week. So it's your choice: Faster-paced/shorter period or slower-paced/longer period.

If you don't enjoy walking (or can't, yet), you can get an exercise video. (I happen to like Richard Simmons' "Oldies" tapes. There are many people in the "show"—and you just dance along with everyone else.) If the music is too fast for you right now, dance at your own pace for a while. If you don't have a VCR, you can put on the radio and dance to the music.

Always begin an exercise session with some easy, mild stretching. Follow this up with a five-minute warmup; do the same exercise you'll be doing, but do it in slower motion, to warm up the muscles before you go into the higher-intensity exercise. After your workout session, you'll need a five-minute cool-down, so the adjustment to your normal activity isn't so abrupt.

"But It Makes My Heart Beat Faster!"

Many people who suffer from panic attacks feel uncomfortable about exercising. They're worried that if they exercise, it will make their rapid heartbeat worse. If this is your concern, you should be aware that a progressively difficult program of exercise will—in the long run—slow down, *not* increase, the heart rate. This happens automatically, through training. So you needn't fear that exercise will make your heartbeat even faster. It won't. It will do the opposite. (Did you know that the average person's resting pulse rate is about seventy beats per minute—while a trained runner's might be only forty?)

Of course, if you're overdoing aerobic exercise—if you work too hard and go into oxygen debt—then, obviously, you're defeating your own purpose. We never recommend too-strenuous exercise. In fact, exercise can trigger the panic attacks, if you overdo. One of our clients was a marathon runner. He ran an average of ten miles a day—and sometimes a lot more. When he cut his practice run down to three miles a day (and improved his diet, too, I might add), the panic attacks stopped.

Exercise, remember, is a stress to the body. Scientists use running as a means of applying stress to laboratory animals when they want to study its effects. They have the animals run a treadmill. But when running is done in moderation, it's a mild stress—and therefore beneficial to the body. Why? Because in adapting itself to meet that stress, the body is encouraged to work better, to perform more effectively.

Some people wonder: How will I know I'm not overdoing the exercise? Won't I have to do a pulse check?

Yes and no. Yes, if you can do it easily—which most people cannot. Aerobic exercise should raise the pulse rate to about 80 percent of your maximum heart rate, which is based on your age. So it involves following a certain formula, learning how to take your pulse—and stopping the exercise while you're doing it, etc.

Too much trouble.

A much easier method is this: Say this sentence aloud, in your normal voice (while exercising): *"I love to exercise because it helps me get stronger and I'll be able to do more things with less effort."* If you can say all that without getting out of breath (i.e., huffing and puffing), you're doing fine. Keep up the good work!

Strength-Training with Weights

Strength-training with weights is also helpful—in addition to your aerobic exercises. If you can possibly get to a gym, that would be the best thing. Just about every gym now has knowledgeable trainers who can guide you through the various exercises you need.

You can start strength-training at any age; it is not just for the young or for athletic types. Here's an interesting study that was done in the mid-1980's. Walter Frontera, M.D., of Tufts University, took a group of volunteers from a local nursing home—ten frail, elderly patients, each with at least two chronic diseases. Most relied on walkers or canes for mobility. They worked at strength-training exercises three times a week, for eight weeks. At the end of that time, these frail, elderly people had increased their strength by an average of 175 percent! These amazing results inspired a host of other clinical trials elsewhere, all of which confirmed the benefits of weight-training.

A book we have found helpful is *Strong Women Stay Young* (Bantam Books, 1998), by Dr. Miriam E. Nelson, also of Tufts University. It contains instructions and how-to illustrations.

How might strength-training benefit those who get panic attacks? Anything that makes you stronger, sturdier, and healthier will help.

An Exercise Game

One day, when the weather was so bad I (SS) couldn't get to the gym, I decided to do my exercise at home. But after a short while, I became bored. I wanted an exercise that was a little more fun, more challenging. Suddenly an idea hit me. What if I turned my exercise session into a game?

From that spark of an idea I eventually developed an exercise game consisting of twenty-five cards. Players shuffle the cards, select one at random, and follow the instructions on it. Each card suggests certain motions—taken from sports like tennis and other activities such as gardening. There are twelve repetitions that you have to do for each of the cards. Players can decide for themselves exactly how to perform the motions and how fast to do them, so there's a lot of room for creativity. After following the instructions on each card, the player is supposed to walk—always within a confined area, so that you can do it inside. The game takes only twenty or thirty minutes, and you'll find you've gotten a really good workout—or should I say playout?

My friends love it, especially those with small children who can play their own version of the game right along with Mom. I play while watching TV.

If you'd like to order my exercise game, please see the last page of this book.

Do a Variety of Exercises

Your muscles work in teams. One set of muscles pulls one way—the opposing muscles pull the other way. So if you do only one kind of exercise, you develop only one member of the muscle team. But by doing a variety of exercises, you get a better-balanced muscle workout—and a nicer-looking body.

Another reason for doing a variety of exercises is that you don't want it to get boring. Exercise is absolutely vital for good health. So make it fun!

"But I'm Too Tired to Exercise"

Very often someone will say, "I know I should be exercising, but I'm just too tired; I have no strength." They reason: If I exercise, I'll only become more tired. But it's just not so. It actually works the opposite way: The more you ask of your body (well, within reason . . .), the more it delivers. A good physical workout will energize you and revive you—because you'll be using your body in an intelligent, healthful way.

Naturally, you mustn't overdo. "Never bite off more than you can chew!" applies to exercise as well as to other areas of life. But you'll notice that as you continue to exercise, as you get stronger, your muscles will just want to do more. You don't have to push yourself; this comes by itself as you train every day.

A Word About Outdoor Exercise

We often see joggers running alongside cars even on the busiest streets and highways, and can't help wondering. These people are presumably doing this exercise for health reasons, yet they're right next to cars that are continually spewing toxic exhaust fumes. When a person does aerobic exercise on a regular basis, his body adapts to the demands: The passages to the lungs expand to take in more air. All this is good; this is why exercise is so beneficial. But if you're jogging (or walking) near traffic, aren't you taking in a lot more polluted air? (The people in the cars are sitting, so their lungs are not working as hard. They're also encased in their own air space, so they're getting less outside pollution.) If you're going to walk outdoors, do it in a park, or at least on side streets, away from cars and buses.

What About Lactic Acid Buildup?

But, you may ask, when you exercise, you're contracting muscle—so doesn't that produce more lactic acid?

The answer is yes, it does. But if you've been exercising aerobically on a regular basis, you've also increased your body's capacity to remove lactic acid. There's a greater oxygen exchange going on now. More blood is being brought to various areas of the body by the exercise itself. More blood brings in more oxygen and carries away the waste. So you're actually neutralizing the lactic acid.

Getting Rid of Anger Through Exercise

Exercise can be put to other uses besides cardiovascular training. It can be used as a muscle relaxant. And it can be used to diffuse anger and frustration.

When you're angry, your hormones scream for action. Yet

civilization (or simple, common decency!) often prevents you from acting. So, let your imagination come to the rescue: Take a pillow and give it the old one-two. Remember—your hormones can't tell the difference between real and not-real. When your mind-imagery shouts, "Take THAT (POW!), you old witch!"—it feels as if it's actually happening. But the blessing is that you needn't feel guilty afterward, because you haven't done anything wrong. You haven't harmed anyone. And, besides, it's just *your* secret. Later, when you're all cooled off, you might talk to that person about why you were angry, if you think it will serve a useful purpose.

Some Commonsense Precautions

- Make sure you check with your doctor before beginning any exercise program.
- Don't continue an exercise program if you are recovering from a cold, flu, or other illness. When you resume exercises again, do so gradually.
- Never overdo! Pace yourself. Work at a speed that feels comfortable for you. "Train; don't strain."
- Always begin an exercise session with a warm-up (a slow-motion routine) to wake up your body gradually. End with a five-minute cool-down (also in slow motion).

CHAPTER 8

Step 4: Attitude

"Virtually all human change begins with attitude."

—*Dr. Wayne Dyer*

Listening to Your Courageous Self

Among our many Selves, we have a dependent, timid Self—and a bold, courageous Self. The timid Self is always crying, "Wh-who me? Oh, no, I c-c-can't," and the bold Self stands up straight, looks 'em in the eye, and declares, "Oh, yes, I can"; "I will; I want to!" Sometimes one voice takes over, sometimes the other. Nobody can be brave all the time—or even most of the time.

But there's a paradox here (how those paradoxes keep cropping up!) and it's this: How that small, timid, dependent Self can have such a strong, loud voice—to drown out that courageous voice! And the courageous voice inside—that foundation of strength—often speaks to us in such a low, meek, soft voice—almost a whisper. (Many times the voice is so low, it can hardly be heard.)

So, your job—if you want to become more courageous— is to strengthen your bold, daring Self. How? By listening for its voice: by encouraging it; by bringing it out more—just as you would encourage a very young, bashful child. (You don't yell at it or criticize or condemn it.) When you *do* hear that little voice, you praise it, you congratulate it!

Obviously, you haven't done all this before. What happened was that you blamed yourself when you lacked the courage to do something. Instead of listening for that inner, daring voice, you became angry at yourself because it didn't speak out loud enough to suit you. But you were the one who criticized it and put it down—who else?

So now you have to allow that courageous voice inside to speak up more clearly, in order to create a proper balance. Just as the parasympathetic nervous system must now be strengthened in order to become equal to the now-dominant sympathetic nervous system, so must the inner courageous voice be strengthened until it can speak just as loudly as the timid voice is speaking now.

Does it sound like a difficult task? It needn't be. In fact, it can be a great, exhilarating experience—if you let it. Each time you do something that you really wanted to do but held back before, because you were afraid—each time you do it anyhow, you'll find it satisfies you on some deep, inner level. Because you've met the challenge—and that's the important thing.

Young animals, including children, seem to be—by nature—endowed with this gift of wanting to do and learn and try—in spite of fear. No—not in spite of. *Because of fear.* Author Richard Bach describes this feeling accurately and with great poignancy:

Remember the challenge of the high board at the swimming pool? After days of looking up at it, you finally climbed the wet steps to the platform. From there it was higher than ever. But there were only two ways down: the steps to defeat—or the dive to victory. You stood on the edge, shivering in the hot sun, deathly afraid. At last, you leaned too far forward. It was too late for retreat, and you dived off the edge. Remember? The high board was conquered in that instant—and you spent the rest of the day climbing steps and diving down.

Climbing a thousand high boards, we live. In a thousand dives, demolishing fear, we turn into human beings.

If we let the "I c-c-can't" voice gain the upper hand, if we give in to it every time it screams, how are we ever going to do anything new?

Doing something new often requires a new way of looking at things. Many people have a fear of contradiction; they fear being inconsistent. So they become stuck in a mold and they can't get out. But what's so terrible about appearing inconsistent? (I remember, at a discussion-group meeting, a man made a statement and a little later, he said the exact opposite. Another man pointed this out to him, accusing him of being inconsistent. And he replied, "So? Where is it written that a human being must be consistent?")

One creative solution to the problem of contradiction is to accept and assimilate both parts—one and the other. In this case, it means accepting the dependent, timid Self as well as the bold, courageous Self. It's important that you make friends with that dependent Self—and not dislike it or reject it (as some of you may want to do), but treat it as a part of your Self, with compassion and understanding. Only then will the strong, more mature part of yourself be able to shine through. (And isn't that another paradox?)

Of course, you don't have to take all this literally—this notion of many Selves residing inside, like little Russian dolls, one within the other. It's just a handy way of looking at this important issue of the two sides of ourselves—the one that wants to hold back and the one that wants to move forward. It's easier to do something about the problem if we view it, in a fanciful way, as two separate voices, each attempting to take over, because then the answer becomes simple: Make that courageous voice louder. Turn up the volume.

We think it would be very helpful to you to do the following exercise. In fact, I (SS) ask all my clients to do this, so we can go over it together and pinpoint exactly where the "trouble spots" are.

Take a piece of paper and draw a line down the middle. In the left column, write down what your dependent, timid Self is saying. On the right side of the page, let your bold, courageous Self answer it. As an example, here's what one client sent me. She and her husband were supposed to go to the Bahamas on vacation, but my client was afraid she'd panic on the plane.

My timid, fearful, dependent Self says:	**My bold, courageous, daring Self answers:**
"I'll be locked in the plane and no one will be there to help me."	"I'm not really locked in: If it were a *true* emergency they *could* land the plane."
"But I need to control something!"	"You can control how you *feel* and *react* to the situation."
"But I hate the panic attacks and I want to fight them before my second fear sets in! The physical symptoms make me feel I'll lose complete control."	"The harder the fight, the further the cure."
"I feel like the thoughts control me, not the other way around."	"Then let them come and pass."
"What about the spacey feeling, the heavy breathing, the dizziness and shaking? I can calm down the symptoms a little, but I can't stop them completely."	"They have no medical significance."

"What if the panic attack doesn't stop?"

"It has to stop eventually."

After receiving this list, I made several comments. I said her answers on the left side sounded real, authentic; the ones on the right side didn't sound very convincing. They sounded like a few memorized slogans. I also pointed out that she couldn't control how she would *feel* in the situation, but she *could* control how she would *act*. She could also control her breathing, since it's partially under voluntary control. And when she wrote she wanted to fight the panic attack *before* second fear set in, I told her that wanting to fight *is* second fear!

I then asked her to re-do this assignment, giving more weight to the answers on the right side of the page; using the pronoun "you" on that side, to make it sound as if it was coming from someone else—a therapist, perhaps, or a very wise friend. She went back to the drawing board, and this is what she sent me:

"Maybe I shouldn't go on this trip. It's safer and more comfortable to avoid the stress of having a panic attack."

"You *want* to go! You love to travel and explore. It makes you feel exhilarated—and you know that! Many people would love to be able to take a trip like this. If you start thinking negatively now, you're only setting yourself up for failure."

"I'm so afraid of something happening to me. I feel it's better to just worry all the time so I'll have my guard up if something bad should happen."

"You are decreasing the quality of your life if you are always worried and fearful. If something is going to happen, keeping a guard up isn't going to prevent it and you will probably be too weary to deal properly with it."

"I feel so disappointed in myself that I have attacks. Why do *I* have to suffer? I just don't feel like full recovery is possible."

"Okay. So you have a problem right now. Many other people have it, too. You are not the *only* one. You can't beat yourself up about it. Don't expect so much. You have been through a lot and you're an extra-sensitive person—which is good. Recovery isn't going to happen instantly, so be patient. Old habits can be reversed, but it takes work and time."

I asked her how she felt after she wrote this new list, and she said, "I felt great! Like I could really do it!"

P.S.: She went on the trip and had a wonderful time. "I'm so glad I was able to go," she told me later.

Many find this step—changing your attitude and negative self-talk—the most challenging step in the program. That's because you've had these ideas for so long that they seem perfectly natural and "logical" to you. Yet to others—who are just as intelligent—they might seem highly irrational. I'm reminded of a line Herman Wouk wrote in one of his novels: "Viewpoint is everything."

If you'd like to change *your* negative viewpoint but don't know how to go about it, or need some help, give us a call at PASS-Group. Either I (SS) or one of my associates will be happy to work with you. Because when you think better, you feel better. This is such an important concept, we'd like to put it up in lights: *Think better, feel better!*

Avoid Negative Chain Reactions

When you try to look at something from a different angle, a whole new train of thought emerges. Because one thought always leads to another. So you can either escalate the panicky feelings (by a train of thought) or deescalate it.

Let's say you're by yourself and you start to think, "I'm by myself." You can turn this sentence in a decidedly negative direction by continuing this way: "I'm all alone. Oh, my gosh, that means if I get a panic attack, nobody will be able to help me. Oh, that would be terrible. I'd be lying there, who-knows-how-long. I'd go crazy. I wouldn't be able to help myself. I wouldn't know what to do. I must have someone with me. Oh, help me, someone, anyone. . . !"

But a different chain of thought might be: "I'm by myself— I'm on my own. But I don't have to worry too much about a panic attack. Because if it comes, I know what to do. And I'm doing it. I'm 'letting go,' getting floppy. I think of what my doctor told me—that I'm very healthy. You know? It's really pleasant being by myself—with no one to bother me. Maybe I'll finish that project I started. Hey, this is going to be fun." (See what I mean?)

Here's another example: "I'm five miles from home." One train of thought can run: "Oh, I've gone too far this time. Now there's nobody around who knows me—I'm all alone—nobody cares what happens to me—what if I get a panic attack here?" (You can guess what happens next.)

But, starting from the same premise, "I'm five miles from home," it can also run like this: "How wonderful that I can travel now—that I'm not bedridden or helpless—that I can enjoy the sunshine today—that I can make my life more interesting now—oh, look at this, I've never seen that before—what an interesting color on that leaf—what a lovely world the good Lord made—and this is all my world, too! It's so good to be alive," etc.

Here are a few more examples: Say, a person fails at something: "I've failed—that's terrible—that means I'm no good— now people won't like me anymore—nobody will care for me—I'll be all alone," etc., etc. Or, he could say: "I've failed. Well, you can't win 'em all . . . But I wonder what went wrong—Why didn't this thing succeed? Was it because of such-and-such? Probably. Or maybe it was because I did such-and-such. Yes, that's it—let's see—oh, I know what I'll try next time—yes, I think that'll work out much better—there; that's settled—yes, I'm sure that'll do the trick—great. Boy, I can hardly wait to try it out next time and see what happens," etc. (Do you see the hopeful note?)

Say a person has a panic attack. He says to himself: "Oh, my goodness, this terrible feeling came over me just now. It must mean I'm going crazy!! Oh, my goodness! Or maybe it's my heart—maybe I'm having a heart attack right now?! Oh, they're gonna have to call an ambulance now . . . ! And I'm all alone here . . . what'll I do?? Oh, this is terrible, terrible!! I think I'll start screaming in a minute . . . Oh, I can't stand it! I'm gonna lose control, I know it! I know it! Oh, what'll I do—? I'm never going to come here again!" etc.

But he can say this instead: "Wow, that left me shaky . . . I wonder what that was all about? Maybe it's trying to tell me something . . . I know I've been under too much of a strain lately . . . I've been trying to do too much . . . and I've also let myself get run-down . . . that's probably what it was . . . I'm just going to have to start taking better care of myself . . . I'm going to eat right, go to sleep earlier from now on . . . get some more rest because of the hours I've been keeping lately . . . and I'll see what happens . . ."

Watch Your Language!

The words you choose when you talk to yourself are very, very important. And it's not just a question of idle semantics: Because words are the tools we humans use to help shape our thoughts.

Many people think (and say) this sentence many times a day: "I can't stand it!"—"it" being waiting on line, being snubbed, not being in charge, or any one of thousands of little annoyances we all endure. But "I can't stand it" is a strong phrase; when said aloud, you can almost feel your toes curl. It's so *final.* It precludes flexibility or acceptance. Those who use this phrase often are (or they soon become) tense, rigid people.

If this sentence keeps cropping up in your vocabulary, you might want to consider changing it to something less formidable, something that expresses your sentiment yet leaves room for change. "I don't like it, but that's the way it is." Or toy with a different concept: "Sure, I don't like it, but what the hell. I can take it; I've got more guts than they think . . ." and so on.

I recently had occasion to talk to one of our former clients, a woman who had taken this program at its very beginning. She hadn't been homebound, but she was very limited in her travel. She belonged to the PTA—and when she'd go to meetings, she would sit way back in the last row, right near the door. (We all know why . . . don't we??) Well, it was a long climb up, but she's in excellent health, enjoys a good social life—*and* she's now president of the PTA!

We spoke about her new life and responsibilities and she told me how much pleasure she derives from having achieved something far beyond her wildest dreams. She told me how, often, when she's on stage, she looks toward the back of the auditorium and marvels at how far she's come. I asked her if she ever gets panic attacks now. She said, "No— but every time I drive by a certain street, I still get a little of that old anxiety feeling." I asked her why, and she said, "Well, that's where it all started, where I first got the panic attack that made me go through four long, miserable years." Both places—the auditorium and that particular street—were strongly associated in her mind with suffering. Yet (as I pointed out to her) look at the difference in her thinking! In one place she's saying things like: "Wow, who would ever have believed I'd be standing up here on the platform . . . ?" And: "I've come a long way, baby . . ." But in the other place, she still sees that street as the start of her "four long, miserable years."

Is it any wonder some of that old feeling creeps back?

One woman called me on the phone recently to find out about the PASS-Group program. She told me she had had a "massive panic attack" about a week before, and that she had been in a terrible state ever since. She had been scheduled to have a laparotomy done because of abdominal pain. (This is a procedure where the doctor looks into the abdomen through a small incision.) This woman had already made arrangements to have someone look after her two children, but on the day she was supposed to enter the hospital, she had the panic attack. In telling me her story, she kept referring to this procedure as "going under." This was the phrase she used over and over again ("I had my children all prepared, but when the day came, I couldn't go under," and "they wanted me to go under"). I pointed out to her the loaded words she was using; she wasn't even aware she was doing it! "Anybody," I said, "would be afraid if they thought they were going under." But what special significance did the phrase have for her, I asked. "Being raped or drowning," was her answer.

The hospital said they'd reschedule her for another day. I spoke to her at length and suggested that the next time she might think of the event as merely a diagnostic procedure— which is exactly what it is. She was greatly relieved. "I'm so glad I spoke to you," she told me again and again. "I feel a lot better already."

Do you see the enormous power that words have?

A Magic Phrase

I once read a story about a paratrooper in World War II. Each time, as he'd jump out of the plane and pull the ripcord, he'd say to himself, in a sort of magical incantation,

"Well, here goes nothing." What he meant was: "Well, so what? This can't be helped. I'm here, I have to do this, I lived my life, it was a good life." So, those few words, "Well, here goes nothing," gave him courage.

Regina (whose story is included in this book), adopted as her motto, "I can do it." Here was a woman, by the way, who was in her mid-sixties. She had suffered from panic attacks for the past twenty years. She could barely leave her home to do the marketing. Many times, she told me, she'd have to sit in the car, unable to leave it, while her husband was in the store, shopping. Then one summer, about a year after she told her story for the book, she and her husband went on an extended vacation trip. They lived in New Hampshire and they drove all the way to Utah to visit their granddaughter. From there, they went to California, then took the southern route back and stopped in Arizona to visit the Grand Canyon. They also went to Washington, D.C., to attend a wedding. Regina enjoyed her trip all the way—she had a ball! How was she able to do it? By following the program and saying to herself (and believing it): "I can do it. I'm well."

Here are a few other examples of what we might call (forgive the pun), "PASS words": One man, who went on to study metaphysics, adopted one of the affirmations he heard about. Before he leaves his house, he says, "I go now to meet my good." One woman is comforted by reciting the Lord's Prayer. Another tells me she says to herself, "I'm surrounded by a healing light." One woman even told me her panic attacks began to go away for good after she told herself, "Hey, this is all a bunch of garbage."

So, you see, anything goes . . .

Try to find a magic phrase of your own that you can say to yourself in moments of stress—that will comfort you, yet, at the same time, give you the courage you need.

There's nothing wrong with this kind of help. In fact, there's everything right about it—from a psychological as well as a physiological standpoint—because you're not relying on drugs; you're relying on yourself. You're relying on your own inner thoughts to bring you peace and comfort. You're drawing on sources of courage and strength that are available to anyone who can read and think and learn.

CHAPTER 9

Step 5: Imagination

"Imagination is more important than
knowledge."
—*Albert Einstein*

Imagination is one of the most powerful of human attributes. Without it, civilization itself would have been impossible. But, like any other powerful tool, it can be used to create—or destroy.

You have an excellent imagination. We know that. (Aren't you always creating, in your mind, vivid disaster scenes?) But why not use this great gift of imagination to help yourself instead of hindering yourself?

The Act-As-If Principle

We talked about how the things we believe in can affect us; how the sentry in the brain can become aroused or calmed by a belief.

But this is the most amazing part: Even if we only *pretend* to believe in something, it can still exert an effect on us.

Do you want to be more courageous? Then *act* as if you have courage.

Suppose you don't feel confident. It doesn't matter. Act the part anyway. Is there someone you know whom you'd like to emulate, to copy? Perhaps a famous person, a teacher—or even the Person-You-Would-Like-to-Become. Just pretend you're that person already.

What purpose does it serve? It can get you over some pretty rough spots. It can also give you a welcome respite from always thinking of yourself and your problems. It can give you a new frame of reference, a new perspective. And the more you act like a confident person, the sooner you'll become one.

One of my clients once told me she was in a situation in which she had formerly experienced great panic. But instead of reacting, she asked herself instead, "Now, what would Shirley have done in this case?" She did it and she was just fine. What *I* really might have done in the same situation is unimportant. What *is* important is that this woman projected, in her own mind, an idealized version of someone else—and pretended that she was that person. And she acted accordingly.

I've used this strategy many times myself. I'd ask, "Now, what would a confident person do?" I'd create a fictitious, confident person in my mind. I'd picture myself as that person. But, as I pointed out to my client, don't forget to give yourself credit for acting well in those circumstances. After all—it was still *you* who did it!

I (SSJ) had switched careers and started my medical training rather late in life. When I graduated from medical school, I was about fifty. Someone asked me, "How were you able to do this at your age?" And I replied, "It was easy. I just pretended I was thirty."

In French, there's a saying: "The appetite comes with the eating." You start with a simple action, pretending, if you have to. And as you continue with the action, things just follow along in the same path. The action picks up momentum. It becomes stronger and stronger.

Once in a while, someone will ask a question like this: "Well, if I act confident when I'm really not, wouldn't that mean I'm denying my feelings? Wouldn't that be lying to myself?"

No, you're not denying your own feelings by acting bravely. You're not pushing down the fear, repressing it, or refusing to face it. On the contrary, you are facing the fact that you have this fear. You freely admit it. But then, you go on to make a conscious decision: Given this fear, what'll I do about it? If I act afraid, my fear will probably intensify. But if I act as if I'm brave, it'll help me and I'll be proud of myself. So therefore, I choose to act with courage. I'll act as if I'm brave. Notice the element of choice here. The person faces the facts (i.e., he confronts his own feelings), and on that basis, he makes a choice.

Applied Fantasy

Fantasy can be a most helpful tool. It allows you to explore new pathways and responses. I use the word *pathways* advisedly. Thinking involves linking neurons with other neurons. And when you do that, you create new patterns—hence new ways of looking at the same thing.

Sir Francis Galton, a British scientist (who, incidentally, was a cousin of Charles Darwin), wrote in 1883 about the important influence of thought and memory in everyday behavior. Real or imaginary sights and sounds, he wrote, can impress themselves on the human mind and mold its reaction. The images can surround a physiological function with an aura of pain or pleasure so vivid, he said, that it can be associated with changed reflexes. Later, of course, Pavlov confirmed this in his famous experiment with the salivating dogs and the bells.

Yes, we all have a rich fantasy life. It's just a matter of putting it to good use. Here are some examples.

When I (SS) was a new driver and still practicing, I had to cross a certain bridge in town. This bridge had a very high arch. I used to call it the Sky Bridge because as you came close, it seemed to go straight up to the sky! I always approached it gingerly. One day, I decided to use fantasy. I pretended I was in the army, driving a jeep. In my mind, I saw myself in uniform—and in my pocket were the battle plans I had to deliver, in person, to the general. The fate of the whole country depended on my getting there in time. As I was driving, my husband (who was with me) suddenly turned to me and said, "Why are you driving so fast?! Slow down!"

One of our counselors advises her clients to think of themselves as a car. A car, she explains, will not run unless it gets proper fuel—and you can't run it indefinitely without some rest. If something goes wrong, a red light goes on to warn you. That means you have to correct those conditions if you want to get good mileage out of your car.

One woman was asked to accompany her child's class on a picnic that involved a boat ride. She was terrified of the boat ride because she wouldn't be in control. (How would she get to shore if she panicked?) In addition to the first aid treatment (just in case), she decided to use the following fantasy: She would become the owner of that boat! Because in her boat, she would be in control. I asked her, "But why stop with one boat? Why not get yourself a whole fleet of boats?" "Sure," she laughed, "why not??" P.S. The trip went very well, no problem. She had a wonderful time and her daughter was happy Mom could come.

Another woman had to go to a party given by her husband's boss. It was to be a very formal affair with many important people present—and she was scared. I happened to mention the story of the woman and her boats—and she decided to use the same strategy: She would own the ballroom! She reported, the following week, that she had a really marvelous time at the party. She walked in, she said, like a queen.

The Olympic Gold Medal champion skier Jean-Claude Killy learned to ski as a small boy. He never had a formal lesson, but he would watch the Olympic skiers in his native village—and he'd imitate them. As he'd ski down the slopes, he pretended he was one of them. And, of course, the day came when he was!

Here's what one client told us: "I was in this store, and I began to feel jittery. Anyhow, I was reaching for my wallet to pay for the things I bought, when I suddenly got this idea. My counselor had always told me to use my imagination in a good way, and also to bring something along from home when I go out. Anyhow, I saw my girlfriend's picture in my wallet—she's this girl I like from school—and I imagined myself being with her. I pictured her scared, and me saying, 'It's okay, I'm here for you. I won't let anything hurt you.' And that's what made me feel better right away. When I thought of somebody else being scared, that helped me forget my own fears. So I've continued to use this same strategy, even when I'd go out driving in the car. I'd stop every now and then, open my wallet, look at her picture, and continue on my way. I don't have to turn back again and run home, the way I used to."

Dr. Toni Grant, the well-known clinical psychologist and radio personality, once offered this fear-reducing technique: Instead of struggling to push the fear out of your mind (which we know doesn't work), simply let go of that effort to drive fear out. But use imagery. Locate the feeling in a certain part of your body. (Where is it—your tummy? Your middle? Your chest?) Then, she said, make that fear bigger; feel that area of your body expand and grow. Know it's only a feeling—and you're controlling it by changing its size. When the area gets large enough, visualize doors and windows in that area of your body. Open wide these imaginary doors and windows—and let the fear escape through these openings. Try it and see if it works for you.

One client told me he visualizes the sentry in his brain as another person who lives inside him. Sometimes, he said, he pictures this person, this sentry, sitting next to him in a chair. In his mind, he talks to him. He asks him what he wants; how they can cooperate together or how he might reassure this sentry.

Sometimes someone will ask: If I talk to myself and fantasize and pretend, couldn't I become crazy? No. As we have pointed out before, psychosis is a whole different ballgame. First of all, in these little head games, you're not substituting fantasy for reality. You're helping yourself cope with reality by redefining it temporarily, to be more in line with the actions you want to assume. And, secondly, you're fantasizing at will.

Come to think of it, aren't billion-dollar industries—the entertainment industry, for example—built around this very concept? Haven't you ever cried, watching a movie or reading a book? You knew the stories weren't real, yet you reacted to some degree as if they were. Of course, the emotional impact isn't as strong as when it happens to us in real life. Nonetheless, something important is going on: Some physical changes are taking place, brain chemicals are being manufactured. Imagination is a powerful force in our lives, for good or ill. We all spend a good part of our day imagining and pretending all sorts of things. We do this because we have a large brain that begs constant input.

Those what-if thoughts you're entertaining all the time (and maybe they're not so entertaining!) are destructive—not because they're fantasy, but because they interfere with your functioning in the real world. Fantasy put to good use, on the other hand, enhances your performance in the real world.

Funny Little "Therapists"

Many of our clients tell us that they were programmed for years to "hear" a negative "voice" inside their heads: "Don't do this . . . stay away from that . . . what will people think . . . what if this, what if that . . ."

One of the best "therapists" around is a fellow named Jiminy Cricket. Remember him from the old Walt Disney movie *Pinocchio*? He's a whimsical little character, about five inches tall; he wears a suit and tie and a high hat, and carries a green umbrella. He can easily perch on your shoulder, and you just carry him around with you, wherever you go. You can project all these negative "voices" on to him—like a ventriloquist. Somehow, when Jiminy Cricket makes these dire pronouncements, they don't sound nearly as threatening as when, for example, it's your mother who "says" them!

"I laughed so hard," a client told us, "when I thought of Jiminy Cricket sitting on my shoulder. You know, I always heard my mother's voice inside my head telling me, don't say this because if you do, they can turn right around and say that to you. Things like that. So that always used to inhibit me. I couldn't speak out. I was always afraid of saying the wrong thing. But now with this little creature on my shoulder, even if he tells me not to say things, he's so comical, I can't take him seriously, and I start to laugh. I find myself speaking up much more these days."

Another client who used to be extremely nervous about driving imagined the Pillsbury Doughboy sitting on her shoulder. Whenever she had to stop for a red light (her "tension-time"), she'd pretend she was poking her finger at his belly-button, making him giggle. This always made her laugh—and relax.

On the Matter of Control

Panic-prone people in general are deathly afraid of "losing control." The solution, they think, is to get a "tight grip on themselves." They want to whip their nervous systems into instant obedience. And they want to be able to diminish the panic attacks through brute strength or sheer willpower.

But, as you've no doubt discovered, this can't be done. In many ways, the emotional brain behaves like a balky two-year-old child. Give it a direct command—and it immediately says no and does the opposite. The more you force and push and strain, the more stubborn the mind becomes.

How do you handle a contrary autonomic nervous system? If brute strength and direct force won't work, what will?

Well, why not try the same strategy that you might try with that stubborn two-year-old? It wants to do the opposite? Fine. Then let it.

One man I remember decided to test this theory in what I thought was a rather dramatic way. He drove at night to a certain street that he hadn't been to in years because of his fear of having a panic attack there. He got out of the car and yelled, "OK, panic attack, here I am. Come and get me!" And you know what happened? Nothing!

I (SS) used to have a bad habit. Whenever I was under stress, I'd make an ugly facial grimace. All my efforts to stop it only made it worse. Then I tried the *opposite* approach—I tried to *make* myself do it. I soon dropped the habit.

One of our clients had difficulty swallowing—and, naturally, she became fearful about the possibility of choking. Three doctors assured her there was no physical abnormality in her throat, yet the difficulty persisted. I explained to her how the autonomic nervous system works, and suggested that she just chew her food and try *not* to swallow. She did that—and, of course, the food went down easily.

Another client had this problem: She would blush whenever she went out in public. To her, this was agonizingly painful, and she practically became a recluse as a result. Again, I explained the paradoxical way the autonomic nervous system works, and how forcing herself *not* to blush would actually bring it on! I advised her to *force* herself to blush instead. She didn't believe me but decided to give it a try, anyhow. The next time I spoke to her, she reported with great surprise that for the first time in years, she didn't blush in the presence of other people. "I tried very hard to blush," she said, "but couldn't!"

There's a school of psychiatry, known as logotherapy, which incorporates as one of its basic tenets this curious phenomenon about the autonomic nervous system. The founder of logotherapy, Dr. Viktor Frankl, called it the "Principle of Paradoxical Intention." But he carried this idea one step further. He instructed his patients to engage in a self-dialogue and *deliberately exaggerate the nervous symptom to the point of absurdity.* For example, if a person was bothered by moist palms due to nervousness, he might say, "My hands are sweaty? Good! I'll show 'em sweaty! I'm gonna fill three buckets full and line 'em up so everyone'll see what a great sweater I am! They'll put my name in the Guinness Book of World Records!" Or: "Am I starting to get 'rubbery' legs again? Fine! I'm gonna make 'em even more rubbery. My legs'll bounce and I'll start jumpin' around like a kangaroo!"

The purpose of exaggerating the symptoms until they appeared ludicrous was to inject a little humor into the situation. We all know that "laughter is the best medicine." Once you can smile or laugh and not take yourself so seriously, your nervousness vanishes.

Hans O. Gerz, M.D., a Connecticut psychiatrist who uses this method with his patients, says, "If I'm seeing a patient who's afraid of passing out, for example, I ask the patient to get up and try to pass out right here in my office. To evoke humor in the patient, I might say, 'Come on, let's have it. Let's pass out all over the place. Show me what a wonderful passer-out you are.' So the patient tries to pass out—and when he finds he can't, he starts to laugh."

So that's one way of exerting control over the autonomic nervous system: Knowing that it cannot be pushed and refraining from pushing it and even making it do the opposite (with humor!).

But there's another way, too. Let me tell you a little story.

There was a famous Russian scientist by the name of Aleksandr Luria who was well known for his work on brain function. His special area of interest was the autonomic nervous system, and he became involved in the study of a man who could apparently control his autonomic nervous system at will. This man was able to voluntarily increase or decrease his heart rate, dilate or constrict his pupils, and so on. Professor Luria wondered: How did this man do it? How could he perform these amazing feats that nobody else could do?

It turned out that the man himself had once stumbled upon a method, which he had perfected through practice. What he would do was invent an appropriate "picture story" to match the effect he wanted to create. For instance, if he wanted to speed up his heart rate, he would imagine he was at a railroad station, trying to catch a train that was just pulling out of the station. He saw himself armed with luggage, running, running, huffing and puffing—and his heart rate would go up. When he wanted to slow down, he'd imagine himself lying comfortably in bed, dozing off, ready to fall asleep. If he wanted to decrease the size of his pupils, he'd imagine a very strong light shining in his eyes, and so on.

This man seemed to be willfully regulating his autonomic nervous system. But, as you can see, he didn't do so directly. He didn't defy any natural laws. He merely used his imagination as a tool to prod his autonomic nervous system to react in a way that he wanted it to react.

So you see, you *do* have control over the panic attacks, although not in a direct, aggressive way.

Dr. Clark's Experiment

Remember our earlier discussion of how giving an infusion of sodium lactate to panic-prone individuals caused them to panic? Dr. David Clark, a British psychologist at Oxford, did the following experiment (which had also been carried out by other researchers, with similar results).

He took a group of panic-prone patients and divided them into two subgroups. One group received the sodium lactate—and 90 percent of the patients panicked. To the second group of patients, however, he said something like this:

"We're going to give you this sodium lactate infusion. Now, this substance is normal to the body; it can't hurt you.

It'll just make your heart rate speed up and your breathing increase. You may even experience some intense sensations during the infusion. But don't worry about it. It won't mean anything is wrong. It's just the effect of the sodium lactate."

And guess what? In the second group, only 30 percent panicked!

This shows that what goes on in the head can override what goes on in the body.

CHAPTER 10

Step 6: Social Support

"Loneliness is something that causes us to take
the risks and to move out. So there's a very *posi-*
tive aspect to loneliness; don't be afraid to feel it."
—*Dr. Leo Buscaglia*

There's no getting away from it: We humans belong to a
social species—which means that in order to remain normal
and healthy, we need the company of others. Naturally, there
are individual differences. Some of us, by nature, are more
outgoing and require more social contact than others. But
we all need some sense of social connectedness, of being val-
ued as a friend, of being socially viable in a positive way.

One of the reasons for the general malaise in our modern
cities and suburbs is the lack of opportunity for many satisfy-
ing social contacts on a daily basis. When you take large
groups of people and you put each one (or each couple) in
an isolated unit; when you stack these units vertically (in
apartments) or horizontally (in private homes) without inter-
connectedness of any kind, surely the inhabitants of these
boxlike structures will experience a sense of deprivation,
especially since, according to one survey, the average American moves fourteen times in a lifetime. It takes much more
effort to make and keep friendships in a society that's so
mobile. But the effort is always worth it.

Fear of Rejection

The fear of rejection seems to be an inborn human characteristic—almost like an involuntary knee-jerk reflex. This has to do with the long history of socialization that our species has gone through. If everybody just did his own thing, without regard to how his behavior affected others, how would mankind ever have formed cohesive tribes and groups?

To an extent the fear of rejection occurs in other species that have been domesticated. A dog, for instance, will tolerate physical pain with great forbearance if he knows his master is on his side. But a dog will cringe in fear (and obvious emotional anguish) if you censure him with cross words or even a black look.

The late Dr. Hans Selye writes in *The Stress of Life* (McGraw-Hill, 1978):

> . . . As much as we thirst for approval, we dread censure. The common statement, "I don't care what anybody says", is almost invariably untrue. Probably I should not have said "almost," because I do not know of a single person who does not care what anybody says. Is this pretense necessary? If a person is quite certain he is right (which is rarely the case among intelligent people), he should stick to his guns no matter how much he is criticized. Many strong people can do this. But no one is indifferent to censure. Why pretend not to care about criticism? Those who are honest with themselves know very well that they would rather be approved than criticized.

So, while a watered-down version of the fear of rejection may be an asset to human development, if carried to an extreme, it becomes a definite liability.

Dr. Rochelle Myers once remarked, "If you don't get rejected at least three times a day, you're not living creatively." She humorously emphasized a very important point:

That being rejected is *not* synonymous with failing. Quite the contrary. In order to live creatively (and who doesn't want to do that?), we must take risks. And when we take risks—when we try new things, when we stick our neck out, when we reach out to others—we *may* be rejected. After all, there are so many people and so many ways of thinking, and so many opinions—that whatever we do, we're bound to step on somebody's toes sometimes. We can't please everyone. So, what we have to do is make allowances for these rejections—and realize that they're only a part of risk-taking. Everyone has to contend with that in one form or another. Why take it so personally? Why get so upset about it?

As I've (SSJ) mentioned, I started my medical training rather late in life. After I graduated medical school, I found it difficult to get a residency because of my age. I figured maybe one out of a hundred hospitals would take me on. So when the letters started coming back saying they wouldn't accept me, I merely kept count. I wasn't unduly concerned about all the negative answers. (Let's face it: I wasn't jumping for joy, either. But I was not unduly concerned.) In fact, the more letters I received, the closer I felt I was to my goal— that letter from the hundredth hospital that would accept me, despite my age. My patience paid off; I eventually did get not one but several letters of acceptance.

The reason I had this positive attitude was because I didn't consider the letters I received as rejection letters. In other words, they weren't really rejecting me, as a person. The negative responses merely reflected the reality of the situation, because, statistically speaking, it *is* harder to secure a position like this at a later age. But harder doesn't mean impossible. And it was nothing personal. So I saw no reason to feel that I failed or that it was my fault. It was this realistic evaluation that helped me stay calm and maintain a positive attitude.

Salespeople have to take something of this stance, too. They have to realize that not everybody is going to buy their products. And they have to set sales goals for themselves that reflect the nature of their product. For example, if you're selling hot dogs in a ballpark, you're going to have many customers in one hour; if you're selling apartment buildings, you may only have one customer a year! Acquiring friends is a little like that, too. If you have one or two real friends in a lifetime, they say, you're ahead of the game!

Many sensitive people, in an effort to spare themselves the emotional suffering of criticism or rejection, withdraw from life. But while this may *seem* to be the less painful solution, in the end they only suffer more—again, because we are basically social creatures. So the benefits are only temporary and short-lived.

Obviously, one way to overcome this is to become more friendly yourself. (You're telling people, in effect, "See? I won't bite!")

The fear of rejection has still another face to it: A person who feels vulnerable and insecure very often dislikes and rejects others who display or remind him of similar traits. (That's why children are often so cruel to their peers. They themselves feel so small and vulnerable.) But the interesting thing is that when a person increases his self-esteem through growth and self-knowledge, he very often becomes much more tolerant—not only of himself, but of others, too.

Even if you're born with a thin skin and are easily hurt and bruised, you have to develop a tougher outside shell, so refusals and rejections don't hurt as much. You can refuse, too—refuse to be hurt or intimidated by a no answer. Simply chalk it up to the law of percentages—and go on from there.

Creating a Bond

There is a constant interaction between any living organism and its environment. The organism will push itself against its environment, so to speak, and the environment will push against the organism. When the environment is too threatening, too overpowering, the organism retreats as a survival measure. On the other hand, if the environment is favorable, if it is approving and permissive, then the organism expands toward the outer limits of its inborn capacity. This applies to all life, from the simplest creatures to man.

Therefore, if you perceive your environment (that is, the people in it) to be hostile and menacing, then it's up to you to find a way out. You cannot expect your soul to expand in a cold, hostile place. Even a plant needs warmth and nourishment. You also need the warmth of a touch, a good word, a stroke now and then. You must form a bond with someone, somewhere. You have to provide an environment in which your soul can flourish.

Don't think this is impossible. There are hundreds of millions of people and animals sharing this planet. Surely, among all those living beings you can find those few with whom you can establish a rapport.

Retreating, withdrawing from life, running away from social contacts and commitments, may seem to be the less painful solution. But in the end, the price you pay for such behavior is enormous. Realize this: The benefits you derive by retreating and withdrawing are only temporary and short-lived. They are not the long-term answer.

Deflecting Attention Outwardly

So many people who suffer from agoraphobia tend to look inward too much, to dwell on minor physical variations of the norm, to notice each breath, each heartbeat. In short: they give in too much to the hypochondriacal tendencies most of us have. Yet, how much more profitable it would be to deflect some of this attention outwardly, to other people, animals, hobbies. To the world of ideas and books. To nature. Science. Literature, art, music, sports. To something outside the self.

One of our clients had a sudden insight one day while riding the subway. "The panic attacks are more apt to come," she wrote, "when you think too much about what goes on inside—and not enough about what goes on outside."

When you deflect your attention outwardly, you not only help get rid of the panic attacks, but you stand to gain an important fringe benefit as well: You become a far more interesting person to be with! And when you meet people in social situations and you start focusing on how to put *them* at ease, it may give you still another fringe benefit. It may make you very popular.

"Stroking"

Some years ago, Dr. Eric Berne, founder of Transactional Analysis, refined the vague term, "social interaction," and honed it down to something specific. He called it "strokes." All higher primates, he pointed out, groom and stroke each other's fur as a means of social communication. We're primates, too—and we have the same need for stroking. But we can do it with words. "Anything that says to another, 'I know you're there, I recognize you,' is a stroke," he said. "These needs are part of our biological and psychological hungers—and these hungers can be satisfied with strokes."

Here's a common, everyday example of what Dr. Berne means. Say you step outside and you see your next-door neighbor. You stop and chat for a while, about the weather—or anything. It really doesn't matter. The important thing is that you've made social contact. So you walk away with that little glow, that sense of being socially connected. It may seem to be trivial. But it's not. It's very important.

Here's what author Donald B. Ardell says—with a little bit of tongue-in-cheek—in *High Level Wellness* (Ten Speed Press, 1986):

Based upon incredibly complicated, extraordinarily scientific, and wonderfully intuitive reasoning, I have personally determined that you need not less than 6.5 hugs and/or warm strokes daily. More than this number will do you no harm; in fact, I recommend you get, and give, as many as you can while getting on with the affairs of the day.

When you get—and give—strokes, you help dispel your anxiety, your tension, your fear. This helps you lower even further your chances of having a panic attack.

Here I must interject a little story that illustrates how far away we've come in our society from the good, ordinary, simple human contacts that many other people around the globe take for granted; and that we, in our rich society, have to painfully relearn.

One of our clients, a young man of nineteen, had been practically housebound when he joined this program. His sister lived about a mile away, in Brooklyn, and when he was able to leave his house more freely, he decided, as one of his assignments, to visit his sister. He was somewhat concerned that he might feel lightheaded or strange while walking, so, in addition to the usual advice about food and relaxation, I also told him to stop to say something to somebody if he feels this way—to ask directions, or the time—just to establish that human contact.

He later told me what happened. He was passing a housing project surrounded by a large open area. He began to feel a little giddy, so he looked around and the only person he saw was an elderly man sitting on a bench near one of the buildings. So my client walked up to him. But when the old man saw this tall, husky teenager in sneakers approaching him, *he* panicked!

Being Able to Trust

Psychologists often speak of the ability to establish trust as one of the hallmarks of the mature person. This may be true—but the question is: Whom will you trust? There are many people out there in the world; there are a lot of good people and there are a lot of bad people. No reasonably intelligent person today trusts everybody, indiscriminately. To think otherwise is quite naive. But since we're social beings, we certainly have to trust some people and establish bonds with them.

Some of you may have been so hurt by someone that you learned your lesson and decided never to trust anyone. But this, too, is an irrational viewpoint. Not wanting to trust anyone is a very painful way to resolve a once-received hurt. If you continue with this viewpoint, you'll only end up the loser—because you'll have missed out on many wonderful friendships along the way. Friends help us achieve a greater degree of security, peace of mind, and contentment.

Even temporary bondings are important, as I told my nineteen-year-old client. I remember, many years ago, having a panic attack in the subway. I was standing holding on to the strap, wondering if I'd ever get out of there alive. A woman who was sitting near me leaned over to me, smiled, and said, "It's all right, dear. Don't worry." Something inside of me immediately relaxed.

Wanting to Belong

Wanting to belong is a very powerful human urge. Yet many people, unfortunately, don't see it this way at all. They see their loneliness as something to be ashamed of, to hide from the world. They don't see this longing for human contact as a normal, human feeling, but as a shortcoming that they themselves must somehow overcome. So they turn even more inward and try to develop their own resources as a substitute for friends.

This, we feel, is a great mistake. Not that you shouldn't develop your own resources—of course you should! But, paradoxically, these can best—or possibly, only—be developed within the framework and context of social interchange and social connections!

I know of an only child (now a happily married young woman) who, in her loneliness in childhood, reached out to correspond with pen pals from all over the world. She still maintains, to this day, her friendships with the girls she used to write letters to, in England, Japan, India, and Australia. She's built up friendships and travel enjoyment for years to come.

Love Rays

Did you know that falling in love makes the body produce more endorphins (the good body chemicals)? That's why we feel so high, so terrific, when we're in love. The whole world is suddenly brighter: The grass is greener, the sky bluer. Even rainy days are shiny. And the little things that used to annoy you don't bother you anymore.

Love, you know, isn't only sexual. It's friendly feelings intensified, a kind of giving. You can not only love your mate, but you can love your friends, your children, your dog, your cat.

I remember my dog, Jenee, a gray poodle. Often, as I'd be sitting in my chair, reading, I'd look up from time to time and catch her staring at me. Such love would emanate from her eyes, it made me think of rays, zapping me with love. Try sending out love rays to some of the people in *your* life, and see what happens.

"What Will People Think?"

Many panic attack sufferers worry a lot about what people will think if they have a panic attack. For that reason they cut themselves off from social life. This is such a mistake! First of all, if you have a panic attack and "control" it the way we're suggesting, others won't even know you're having it—unless you choose to tell them. Secondly, if people see you're doing something to help yourself—if you're going out, if you're keeping active, if you're following a program—they will be a lot more sympathetic and try to help, too. But if they see you doing nothing, if they hear you whining and complaining, they will certainly not be as sympathetic. And who can blame them?

You see, we *all* have to overcome fear of one kind or another. We all pay our dues, so to speak. So people don't like to see others getting off scot-free. It's as simple as that.

Starting a Social Network in Your Own Neighborhood

It's really not that difficult to start a social network—once you put your creative talents to work! Almost all communities, however small, have a newspaper—and you can place a small ad there. Not to advertise overtly for friends; that would be so obvious that it wouldn't work! Instead, you might start a special interest group around your hobbies and interests. For example: a sewing club; arts and crafts; baby-care club (where you read and discuss appropriate books); general discussion club; gardening club; weekly religious readings; and so on.

Your ad might simply read: "Needlework Club"—or whatever—and give your telephone number. (If you're reluctant about inviting strangers into your home, you can screen the calls when they answer the ad.) All you need to start a club are just two other people. I (SS) started a very successful neighborhood Discussion Club using this same method. Two people answered my ad—and from this small beginning, the Club grew to a dozen members, and it lasted a good number of years.

I knew a woman who started a sewing club in the apartment building where she lives. One day, she tacked a notice about the club near the mailbox. Two tenants responded. One tenant had a friend in a nearby building who was interested; the other knew of a relative. So little by little, the group grew in size.

About a year later, I went to a local art show and was delighted to meet this woman again at one of the booths. By then, the group had become professional. They were all making beautiful projects, such as needlework and dolls. The entire group's work was on display, and many of the items were for sale. This woman—the founder of the club, who once suffered from phobias—told me she felt great. And why not? She had new friends, new interests, and a much healthier attitude.

Your meetings might be held in members' homes on a rotating basis. You can plan to have weekly, bi-monthly, or even monthly meetings. This outlet can afford you great pleasure and be a source of an increasing network of friends.

From there, you can branch out to other areas. Once you become more mobile, many other opportunities will surely present themselves: other clubs to join, classes to attend, and more. Your interests will by then be directed more outwardly, so you'll be hearing a lot more about these community activities.

The main thing is to recognize how important it is to have a social network.

Our "Anti-Stress" Club

I once organized a neighborhood "anti-stress" club, whose purpose was to get together with other women, not only as a social club but also to help each other with problems as they arose.

One day, we were all sitting around my big kitchen table. One of the women brought up her problem: She couldn't ride on buses. Someone asked her why, and she said every time she got on a bus, she'd get a panic attack. That was why she stopped going on buses. I asked the women in the group—there were ten of us at the time—if anybody had ever had a panic attack. Slowly, every hand in the room went up.

We looked at each other—and burst out laughing. Here we were—a group of normal, average neighborhood women—yet each of us had experienced episodes of unprovoked panic! Unless there was something wrong with the Law of Averages, I thought, this problem is very, very common. Yet, each of us thought we were the only ones. And we were ashamed to admit it: "What would people think?"

And what became of the woman who was afraid to go on the bus? She was instantly cured! The bus episodes had happened to her some years before—and all this time she avoided buses. Our meeting happened to be on a Tuesday; every Wednesday she went to play bingo. But the following day, her husband was unable to drive her there. She decided to go anyhow—by bus. She figured: If panic is so common and everybody has it, why should I worry? So she went and had a very enjoyable evening. Ever since then, she has never minded having to take the bus.

There's even an addendum to the story: She also got over her fear of flying. Several months later, she went down to Florida—for the first time—to visit her mother.

We had many other success stories in our anti-stress club. One of our members, Rose, had a great fear of driving—although she did have a driver's license. She was a widow, and for the four years since her husband had died, she had been totally dependent on her sister to drive her to the supermarket, the doctor's office—everywhere. Meanwhile, her car was right there, in the garage; nobody was using it. The crisis came when her sister (who lived in the same building) planned to move to another state, where her daughter lived. Rose felt cornered; she was terror-stricken at the thought of having to drive. What we did at the club was this:

One of the members who lived several blocks away decided to hold a little party. The plan was to have Rose drive—by herself—to attend the party. A few people that Rose knew were invited to be the mystery guests. On the day of the party, just before leaving her house, Rose called me for reassurance, as we'd planned. Then she called the woman who was holding the party. Rose knew there'd be a surprise for her, but she didn't know what. That was part of the lure, the magnet, to get her to the party.

When she arrived and rang the bell, there was a little welcoming group: "Surprise!" The house had been decorated. There was food and music. They all had a wonderful time. Rose drove by herself (as planned)—and that day marked the end of her fear of driving. This happened years ago, and Rose is now driving everywhere.

Another woman, Ellen, developed a fear of having guests come to her house. It seems that her husband, a very gregarious, outgoing fellow, used to invite people to come up for coffee all the time. Ellen was brought up in a household where they rarely had visitors. So she never learned the art of being a good hostess. She always felt inadequate around guests—simply because she didn't quite know what to do, how or what to serve.

So we helped her. We came to her house as guests, and Ellen practiced serving us. We did this twice—and she successfully overcame her fears. Ellen mastered the new skill, and she no longer had to quarrel with her husband when he brought home unexpected company.

Self-Help Groups

Although I (SS) only do one-on-one telephone counseling at this time, a number of people have asked me whether I think self-help groups are effective in helping panic attack sufferers.

I have to say that it depends on the group and its leader.

I was once invited to sit in on a group therapy session for people who had phobias. It was supposedly led by a professional psychologist. I say supposedly because all he did was sit in a corner and take notes. One man (who loved to hear himself talk) dominated the conversation with complaints about his "impossible mother-in-law." You can't have a successful group meeting when somebody dominates the conversation like this.

In order to be an effective, successful group, there has to be the generation of positive energy. When people see others getting better; when they realize there's hope; when they begin to view themselves as part of a group and not alone anymore—so many good things begin to happen in the group. On the other hand, there are some people (fortunately, a small minority) who are filled with what I can only call negative energy. They simply drain you. They don't really want to get better—or help others to get better. Instead, they want to draw everybody down to their level—and make others feel as miserable as they feel.

People who are susceptible to panic attacks are very suggestible—especially when it comes to "new" symptoms. That's why you need a very good leader who can steer the group's attention toward recovery and encourage members to help each other, working as a team. Also, the group must have a focus and a plan.

One of my former clients started a successful nonprofit organization in North Brunswick, New Jersey, called Panic Relief. Using the seven steps of the PASS program, she started with one group—and now has eight "satellite" groups all over the state. Other organizations use the twelve step program of A.A. as their focal point.

So you do need a good guide and good leadership for a group to be successful.

CHAPTER 11

Step 7: Spiritual Values

"The fruit of faith is courage."
—*Shirley Swede*

To me (SS), the spiritual values are the good, meaningful, important things in life. We can neither touch them nor measure them. And yet they affect our lives in very profound ways. I'm talking about such things as love, beauty, hope, courage, and faith.

Courage

Each culture, each civilization, takes the raw material of human clay and shapes it to its needs. It's not that human nature can be changed; it can't. It's just that each society draws out and magnifies certain human traits, while, at the same time, it subdues and inhibits others.

In the olden days, when bravery on the battlefield was absolutely necessary for victory, courage was amply rewarded. And wherever it was rewarded and admired, many became motivated to cultivate courage in themselves. If you've studied ancient Greece, you'll remember the city-state of Sparta. The Spartan way of life was harsh to the extreme. Its people were tough as nails. Self-discipline, bravery, and courage were overemphasized, while the gentler, artistic aspects of life were sharply suppressed. This is not to say, of course, that societal extremes are to be admired; they're not. But we merely want to point out how malleable human beings are and how they can be molded by society.

History records that the Spartans were fearless fighters. But this isn't entirely true. They were human beings, like the rest of us. They, too, were afraid of danger, death, fire, and so on. But they were taught, from early childhood, to act with courage and stoicism in the face of fear. And, in time, they developed traits of courage and daring until these became second nature to them.

But what happens in our society today? In an age of push-button warfare, governments don't particularly need courageous citizens. In fact, courage is a hindrance to the politicians; they'd much prefer a docile, submissive population. Nowadays, when people do display acts of courage—as, for example, when someone sees a crime being committed and rushes in to save the victim—is such a noble act rewarded? Not only isn't it rewarded, but the hero is sometimes punished for his heroism! (He has to appear in court to testify; lose time from work; face possible revenge by the released and angered criminal; and so forth.) Thus, unintentionally perhaps, the noble trait of courage is quietly suppressed. People begin to look the other way. After a while, people become indifferent.

Yet courage can't become extinct altogether. It's a trait that was built into the human organism through countless generations of evolution, when our ancestors were forced to do battle with the Ice Age and saber-toothed tigers. Courage is there, in each of us. A little dormant, perhaps, through years of slumber—but it's there. And it can be brought out again and developed—*if* the individual wants it so.

How do you develop courage? Just as you would any other trait: First you have to want to acquire that trait. Then you have to practice it.

What does courage mean? Is it the absence of fear? Is it not giving thought to danger?

No. Courage is the willingness to do something difficult—*despite your fear*—if you know it's for an important or worthwhile goal. *There's no such thing as courage without fear.*

As an example, say a soldier is walking across a minefield, but he doesn't know it's a minefield. He thinks he's walking across a meadow. Is he exhibiting courage? No. (Well . . . unless he happens to have agoraphobia . . .) But if the soldier *knows* there are mines there and he still goes, despite the danger, because that's what he has to do—well, that takes a lot of courage.

Fortunately, few of us are called upon to walk a minefield in our daily lives. Yet personal courage is just as important for us as it is for the soldier.

We also have to know how to apply courage, because, like any other trait, it can be misdirected and misused. Take, for example, the white-knuckle flier. A person who goes on a plane trip, fearfully holding on to himself, hour after hour, is certainly showing courage—but it's the wrong kind. It's not necessary—because there's a better way.

As Dr. Weekes writes: "Recovery is not built on knowing you had the courage to board the bus and sit through hell with clenched teeth . . . recovery lies in learning to sit in the bus with the right attitude."

- When your fight-or-flight instinct is aroused and you get that urge to run away—*but* you know that feeling is only temporary and that the best way to handle it is to relax and not run;
- When you start those what-if thoughts—*but* you know you should be turning all those what-ifs into a cheerful "so what";
- When you really want to go somewhere and that little voice starts to say, "What if I go there and get a panic

attack and make a fool of myself in front of all those people?"—*but* you know you should answer, "The hell with that . . . who cares?"—and you go anyway . . .

That's showing courage!

Forgiveness

Forgiveness means letting go of the hurts of the past. It means forgiving others for some of their mistakes, their shortcomings. Often you have to let time pass before you can do this.

Most important, forgiveness means forgiving yourself. For past mistakes, for not getting well sooner—whatever is relevant in your case. If you've hurt someone, don't be embarrassed to say you're sorry; it will bring you peace. A true spirit of forgiveness will wash away much of your suffering and pain and help you recover.

Hope

Hope is a very powerful emotion. It's one of the strongest positive emotions we have. Even love, which we think of as another powerful emotion, has undertones of hope in it. When we're in love, we look at another person and see ourselves already happy, already walking off together into a glorious future. So—when you stop and think about it—it's really hope—not so much the immediate feelings of admiration and tenderness—that makes failing in love such a beautiful experience for us. Hope is what gives our inner chemistry that strong boost—like a shot of amphetamines. And suddenly everything in the world becomes marvelous and bright.

We used the phrase, "like a shot of amphetamines." But it's more than just a metaphor. A chemical very much like amphetamines is released in the brain—and it's this chemical (actually, a combination of chemicals) that gives us that high when we're in love, when we're hopeful.

So science again is reaffirming what we've known all along: That hope, love, trust, and faith are real and solid, not just ethereal things-of-the-mind. These emotions can and should be evoked as often as possible, so that the body's chemistry can correct itself and re-create that harmony between the stress chemicals and the good chemicals that we spoke about earlier.

Unfortunately, in our society, things like hope, courage, faith, and trust—in other words, the spiritual values—are not stressed enough. They're not part of everyday life. In fact, just the opposite is true: The negative is what you hear most in the media—alcoholism, drug abuse, crime, wars.

No, we cannot control the outside world. But we do have some measure of control about what goes on in our own minds—not by stifling information and saying, "Oh, I mustn't think about it" (you know by now that's not the way), but by filling your life with music, art, loving, dance, friends—and all the beautiful things you want to happen to you. If you take these into your life, if you think about these things and make them a part of your daily habits, they'll exert an effect on your life. So, the positive input will replace or neutralize some of the negative input. And more of the healing process will take place.

How do you encourage your body to produce more of these feel-good chemicals? By putting yourself—bodily—into situations where such emotions can more easily be generated. You do this by setting your life up so that you maximize the opportunities your body has to manufacture these good chemicals. When you exercise, you do that; when you eat good foods, you do that; when you balance your work with play, you do that; when you're in the company of good friends, you do that—and so on. You may not be able to control everything, but you can set things up so the chances of a successful outcome will be very high.

For example, if feelings of faith and trust can be evoked by hearing a Sunday sermon, by all means, go to church. If feelings of hope can be fanned by reading inspiring books, by all means, read inspiring books. If you get a lift when friends come over to sit and chat, by all means, make your home inviting and pleasant—so people will want to come over and visit you. This is your responsibility to yourself.

Do faith and trust come first—and then the body starts making the good chemicals? Or is it the other way around? I think this is a little like the chicken-or-the-egg question. It doesn't matter much which comes first. The pattern is a circular one.

Faith

Faith can take many forms. It can be interpreted by each of us according to our own experience, our own background and belief.

A professor once told me that he thought trusting your body and mind meant "allowing yourself to be restored by your own inner mechanisms." I liked that answer. After all, when a doctor treats a person, what he does is adjust or arrange favorable circumstances so that the body's own ability to heal itself can take over. Isn't this how the doctor treats a broken leg? All he does is align the bones the right way— and nature takes care of the rest. The doctor himself doesn't knit the bones together. The inner mechanisms do that. Machines can't repair themselves, but our bodies and minds can. Exactly how this works is beyond our understanding. Yet our job is to trust this life-force within us. And as we do, we reaffirm our faith.

We're not talking here in a strictly religious sense—one need not be a religious person in order to experience faith. Even a scientist who happens to be an atheist must operate from the vantage point of faith: He knows that when he mixes several chemicals together, they will always yield the same compound; that the stars are there even if he can't see them; that the scientific principles he discovers today will still hold true tomorrow.

But we also have to have more faith in our bodies, in our minds, in ourselves. If you haven't walked down Main Street, or been to the center of your town, in years, it requires a leap of faith to open the door—and walk out.

Yes, it's sometimes difficult to trust, to have faith. But it's even more difficult without them.

Naturally, we're not presuming to tell you what to believe in. That's between you and your conscience, as they say. What we are suggesting is that a belief in something of value, something greater than yourself (or your fear), is an essential component in the development of a serene and tranquil attitude.

PART III

PREPARING FOR ADVENTURE

CHAPTER 12

Making Your Trip More Enjoyable

"Life is either a daring adventure—or it is nothing."
—*Helen Keller*

Motivation

One of my (SS) clients once told me, at the end of our counseling sessions together, that now she felt comfortable to go "all over, except—" and she mentioned the name of the next town.

"What's in the next town?" I asked.

"My mother-in-law lives there."

"Do you want to visit your mother-in-law?" I asked.

"No," she admitted.

Motivation is a key that can open up many doors. Here is an example. One of our clients, Alice (whose story is included in this book), lived in Vermont. Her greatest wish was to be able to come to Brooklyn to visit her family. I (SS) was her counselor and I also happened to live in Brooklyn.

Alice was in the program just about the time of the Brooklyn Bridge Centennial celebration. At one point in our sessions, I felt she was ready to make the trip—and I told her so. Her first reaction was, "Oh, no—not me, not now. I'm not ready yet." But I knew she was. So I began sending her leaflets about the celebration, which described Brooklyn in glowing terms. That was to get her to build up an appetite, to become more mentally ready to go. And it worked. Each time she demurred a little less. Then Alice wrote a letter to her family in Brooklyn, telling them that maybe—just maybe—she might be coming to see them. Well, letters flew back and forth; everyone became excited about Alice's visit. This momentum picked up its own rhythm, and culminated in a wonderful adventure. Not only for Alice, but for her family as well.

If you're finding it difficult to venture out, to get going, you're probably using the wrong approach. You probably daydream of a Magic Day, when you'll wake up one morning and find you're suddenly transformed into a person with a desire to go to such-and-such a place. Well, it's a nice dream. The only problem is—that's not the way it happens.

Inertia, the wish to let things remain the way they are, is a very powerful force in our lives. It's as true with people as it is with physics. A person would much prefer NOT to change unless there's a strong force—most often an outside force— that *pulls* him away from the status quo; that *draws* him away from A to B because he wants to be at Point B.

If you want to do something and there is no "outside force" to compel you, then you have to create it yourself. You have to find, in the place you want to go, a sort of magnet that will draw you there; lure you; beg you to come.

Sure, it's easy to just sit back and daydream, "Yes, some day I'll do such-and-such." But if the wish is too vague and fuzzy, then, of course, it won't work. Napoleon Hill, the well-known author, understood this perfectly. "There is a difference," he said, "between wishing for a thing and being ready to receive it. No one is ready for a thing," he added, "until he believes he can acquire it. Until he has a burning desire for it. The state of mind cannot be merely hope or wish."

If you can't get going on your own, you may mistakenly consider yourself weak. Or think you have no willpower. But this isn't fair to you. You're not being weak. You're just using your mental resources incorrectly; you're working with the wrong set of tools. You have to understand that the mind needs a goal, an incentive; otherwise, it doesn't budge.

So, in order to change and start moving, you have to put a carrot in front of the donkey.

If you don't have a carrot, you have to scrounge around until you find one. Because it's up to you to arrange the circumstances that will allow this to happen. If you don't do it, Life does it for you. But you have to wait, in that case. And who knows how long?

It reminds me of a woman I once knew. She absolutely refused to travel beyond her limit, which was a 100-mile radius from her Brooklyn home. When her husband suggested a trip to another city, she'd measure the distance on the map—and if it was, say, 102 miles, she wouldn't go. She told me she'd been that way ever since she was a girl. When her son moved to another state, she wanted very much to visit him—but she couldn't go; it was too far. She had lost her husband some years before, and she lived near a sister to whom she was very close. Eventually the sister and her husband moved to California. It was only then that she finally decided to ignore her 100-mile limit. And for the first time in her life, at age seventy, she boarded a plane and flew to California.

So you see how motivation works? Without a lure, without a bait—something to coax you, to make you want to do it—nothing gets done. You can say from here until tomorrow, "Oh, how I'd love to go to such-and-such a place," but you won't go there unless you find the magnet that will draw you there.

So, the next time you plan your trip, make it interesting, exciting. Plan to do something that you really enjoy. This will give you the necessary impetus to get you out of the house.

Pleasurable Tie-ins

The aim is to build up new and pleasurable associations with the once-dreaded fear-place. By tying in something pleasant with a formerly unpleasant task that must be done, you're establishing a much less formidable situation. It's almost as if the two—the plus and the minus—cancel each other out, and the result is a neutral acceptance, which may later turn out to be a real pleasure.

Here are some examples of how little pleasures can ease big burdens:

One woman in the program ties in her love of opera with her fear of driving. She keeps cassette tapes of her favorite operas in the car, and listens as she drives. A young woman who used to dread waiting in line at the supermarket now picks up a magazine at the checkout counter and happily reads about Hollywood goings-on while awaiting her turn. One woman who used to worry about standing on an open platform to wait for her train now buys an evening paper to make her wait more pleasurable. Another young lady, whose fear was elevators, memorizes jokes in the elevator from little index cards she carries with her. She's well on her way to becoming the life of the party with her repertoire of jokes. One woman brings her knitting along. When I (SS) go on extended trips, I also like to bring along some handwork to do. On one trip, I brought along my crocheting and a little bag of many-colored yarn. I can still remember how comforting this was to me, to look at all the exciting colors and to design the placing of these granny squares. Years later, I still enjoy the blanket I made then.

One of our clients, a woman who lives in a very small town, had to drive her sister to the nearest large city to undergo a medical procedure. The hospital was about a hundred miles away. She was very nervous about that long trip. I advised her to prepare beforehand by choosing three topics of conversation for the car ride, based on some childhood experiences. The topics I suggested were: "My Happiest Childhood Memory," "An Embarrassing Experience," and "The Time We Put Something Over On—." She told me afterward that the long drive turned out to be a very pleasant experience (and this despite the seriousness of the situation itself). The woman and her sister felt so much closer to each other, she said, sharing and remembering childhood experiences. They even stopped on the way back to visit a country fair. And no panic attacks!

So you see, you don't have to grit your teeth and bear it. There are so many ways to make your trips or experiences enjoyable!

Once, when I was talking to a client who was planning her first trip downtown, she said to me, "Never mind about making the trip more enjoyable—I'd be satisfied just to get there!" And I answered, "But that's the whole point! It has to be made more enjoyable if you want to get there."

You have to dangle a carrot in order to move the cart.

All at Once

Some years ago, an ad appeared in a woman's magazine picturing a kitchen sink with a stack of dirty dishes that reached the ceiling. A horrified housewife was surveying the mess. I forgot what it advertised, but the caption read something like this: "How would you like to wash a year's dirty dishes all at once?" Yet some people want to be able to do just that! They want to do *all* their work at once; they want to see the *whole* road they're traveling *all* at once; they want to have everything *now, all* at once.

Maralyn L. Teare writes, "I observed, while working with phobic people, that there is a direct correlation between length of gaze and symptom level. What this means is: The farther the person looks into the distance and the more that is consumed visually, the higher the symptom level." Sight, she points out, is our chief sense and provides us with more environmental information than any of our other senses. Therefore, it's the most important single factor in keeping the brain busy. In addition, looking ahead implies contemplating the future: "What will happen when I'm at Point A?"

When I (SS) was first learning to drive, I was overwhelmed by the traffic around me. I looked at all the cars coming from the other side and wondered about a head-on collision: What if one of those cars crossed over to my lane? My driving instructor told me to concentrate on my own lane, to watch the space in front of me, and to think about where *I* was going. In other words, to mind my own business and not try to see all the roads at once.

When I did that, my driving improved. When you limit your attention to the task in front of you and stop trying to see everything—past, present, and future—all at once, your level of nervousness goes down.

Does this mean you shouldn't plan? Of course not. You plan the overall setting; then you relax, and direct your attention to what's at hand.

Testing, Testing

Many people who first venture out to new places or try new things go with the mental attitude of testing themselves. We think this is the wrong attitude. Think back to when you were in school: Remember test day? How everyone was so nervous? So you're putting an extra burden on yourself when you consider the things you do as a test. It conjures up that old critical self again, the one who always watches you with such a grim expression. It can throw a damper on any experimentation or innovation you might want to try.

Think of it, rather, in these terms: You've already learned to use a number of tools or techniques. Take one of the seven steps, for example: imagination. You can fantasize. You can pretend you're someone else—or somewhere else. When you make the situation different and better, you lessen the impact of the experience. You can do the QR. You can allow gravity to tug at your sleeves and pull at your muscles, to relax them. You can slow down and breathe diaphragmatically. Instead of thinking of the coming adventure as a test, pretend you're the doctor—a surgeon—with a nurse standing by, holding a trayful of instruments (tools) and *you* select whatever tool you need to carry out your assignment.

This mind-set will help you think about all the knowledge you've acquired, all the things you can do. Isn't it better to see the situation you're about to encounter as a place to play with your newfound tools—as an opportunity to experiment with them?

If you haven't done something in a while—or if you're doing something for the first time—of course you're going to feel "strange" or a bit apprehensive. That's only normal. (Sometimes after recovering from the flu and going out "for the first time," it can feel strange the first day just being outdoors again.) So give yourself time to get adjusted.

A Trip to the Beach

It may take a little planning to prepare for a trip the right way, but the results will be well worth it.

Here, for example, is what one client told us:

My goal, when I started the PASS program, was to be able to truly enjoy a vacation with my family. So I'm going to tell you what happened this time when we went on vacation.

I was always terribly afraid of bridges (among many other things!) because I'd always get a panic attack whenever I crossed a bridge. I used to worry all the time: What if I get stuck there and can't leave? Anyhow, my family wanted very much to go to the beach (another place for panicking). But in order to get there, we had to cross a very long bridge.

We left on a Friday, about 4:30 or so in the afternoon. There was myself, my husband, my two children—and each of the kids brought along a friend. We went in two cars; it was a four-hour drive. The thing that had really been worrying me about this trip was the fact that this was my first big trip since I joined the program. So it was like the first time out. Then, there was that bridge (a *drawbridge,* yet!).

I had prepared for it exactly as the program suggested. I looked up material about the bridge in the encyclopedia, and I began to think of it in a factual way rather than in an emotional way. I began to replace myths with facts. I used to worry about the light on the bridge: What if it turned red and we had to stop? But I realized there's a reason for the light. The bridge has to open up so a big ship can go through. So you just have to wait there patiently until it's your turn to go. I kept that in the back of my mind. And I really started to feel calmer when I would think about it.

Until the day of the trip! Then, all these negative things were just assaulting my mind. And it was then that everything was blown out of proportion—like the bridge was going to be a million miles long! But, anyway, I packed the food; we piled into the car, and took off.

It was dark, so I couldn't do any knitting or reading. I just "acted as if." I was doing all the right things outwardly—or inwardly, I don't know which—but I wasn't totally relaxed all the time. Intermittently, I kept hearing in my mind the relaxation tape and then I'd feel waves of relaxation going through me. And so I stayed pretty relaxed. I didn't at any time lose control as far as getting a panic attack, but I wasn't as totally relaxed as I would have been sitting at home. I just continued to "act as if," going through the motions, and doing all the right things I knew I should be doing. Yet, from time to time, I'd be thinking: Bridge-bridge-bridge.

Well, we finally reached the bridge. So, here's the bridge in view, and here we are, traveling right up to it. And I'm thinking, "Oh, there's the bridge!" Then, we came on to the bridge, and I didn't have any panic at all! It was so nice—that bridge was beautiful! I looked down at the water and I just loved it! When we got off, I wanted to go on that bridge again! That was the best time I ever had. I was thrilled and amazed. But I was also proud of myself because, at the same time, I had all those other past experiences to compare it with. And here I was—I looked over the ocean, down near the bridge, and I said to myself, "Gosh, isn't this the most beautiful, breathtaking sight?" Whereas before, I used to hold on to the car, gritting my teeth and being panicky all the way over any sort of bridge, even a small one.

As I told my husband afterward, that was a really big hurdle out of my way. And it was the first time in my whole life that I enjoyed the beach. Before, the openness and the sound of the waves—they were sort of "outside" things, while my own mind felt sort of dark and scary. (I don't know how else to explain it.) So I never enjoyed the beach. But this time it was totally different: I loved it! In fact, the whole experience was great! Coming back on the bridge, I felt the same thrill and happy excitement as before. So I think I'm just doing great!

Dress for Success

When first venturing out, the tendency is to focus more on how you feel and not necessarily on how you look. So you end up wearing "any old thing," thinking it doesn't matter.

Yet we all know that when we look better, we tend to feel better, to think better, to have more confidence.

I'm (SS) reminded of what Gen, one of our PASS-Group counselors, once told me. She had a new client who was homebound. When I asked her how this client was doing, she told me, "Oh, fine. She's going out now."

I was rather surprised because this was only their second or third phone session. I asked her how she did it.

"Oh, I just gave her the high heel treatment."

"High heel treatment?" I asked. "What's that?" And she recounted the conversation that took place:

GEN: I bet I know what you're wearing. You're wearing an old bathrobe and you've got no makeup on.
CLIENT: Uh—how did you know that?
GEN: Look, I want you to get all dressed up—high heels, a fancy dress, earrings, the whole bit. And I want you to put makeup on—lipstick, eye shadow, everything.
CLIENT: But I'm only going to be sitting home.
GEN: It doesn't matter. You can sit home. But I want you to get all dressed up anyway. It's part of the treatment.

As you've no doubt guessed by now, when her client got all dressed up, she didn't feel like sitting home alone anymore. So she went out. Her clothes put her in a different mood.

So clothes *are* important. They do make a difference in the way we feel—and therefore, in the way we *act*.

Eighteen Ways to Make Your Trip More Enjoyable

1. Have a definite, pleasant destination. Don't just go for the sake of going . . . or to test yourself. (Very few socalled normal people would relish the thought of going

out without a specific destination or purpose.) So, visit a friend . . . go to the library . . . browse around a card shop . . . buy something, etc.

2. If at all possible, have a friend meet you at your destination or at a halfway point, to complete the trip together. If that's not possible, call up a friend before you leave the house *and* when you get to your destination. Make it a shared experience.

3. By all means, *plan* your overall trip before you start. But also make allowances for the unexpected. Look forward to small delights: colors, sounds, experiences. It'll make your trip far more interesting than if you try to plan each little detail in advance (it never quite works out that way, anyhow).

4. Realize this: The chances of something bad happening on this very trip are—statistically speaking—very, very slim indeed! So why spoil your trip with unnecessary worry?

5. Have an enjoyable errand to do. Example: if you're going visiting, bring along a small gift. If you're going to a store, buy a little something. If you're going for a walk, be prepared (mentally) to enjoy the street scene, gardens, whatever.

6. Make sure you're as well or appropriately dressed as possible. Wear something new if you can. It'll give you a lift. Women should wear makeup.

7. Bring along some food (complex carbohydrate plus protein). Don't rely on what's out there (otherwise, you'll probably end up with a chocolate bar).

8. Greet neighbors with cheerfulness and enthusiasm. Get into a positive social mood (put on an act, if you have to!). Smile—or better yet, laugh—before you even open the door.

9. If it wouldn't make you feel foolish, it's quite all right to take along a security blanket or good luck charm—a let-

ter, medallion, penny, etc. (But don't choose overt props that you can hide behind—like an umbrella or dark glasses.)

10. If you seem to have a lot of nervous energy ready to pounce out of you, think of it as excitement, which it is, rather than nervousness. Words can have strong positive or negative connotations. "Nervousness" is such a negative word; "excitement" a positive one. So you might as well express your feelings in a positive way. *Remember:* Everyone experiences a heightened sense of excitement when they do something new. Many people find this excitement highly pleasurable—that's why they're always eager to try something new, to visit new places. So don't become unduly concerned if you're experiencing more excitement than usual. It's perfectly normal.

11. Have something enjoyable to do during the trip. Example: If you're on a bus, read, crochet, solve a crossword puzzle, study faces, write a poem, etc. If you're out walking, admire the gardens on the way. Whenever possible, stop to chat with someone. Be friendly.

12. See yourself as very much a part of the Universe, a product of our planet Earth. Feel that sense of connectedness with all living things. Know that we have common roots that reach far, far back in time.

13. Remember, as a child, watching the moon from a moving car? How it seemed to move along with you wherever you went? Make yourself the center of your little world, pulling everything along with you wherever you go. "Wherever I go, that's where I am," says Dr. Wayne Dyer.

14. As you walk (or sit in a car), *let go* of all muscles not in use. Make those muscles as slack as possible. Even when they seem quite relaxed, make them even more "floppy."

15. As soon as you begin to experience more excitement than is comfortable for you, do the QR.
16. Don't go jumping too far ahead of yourself. Don't try to see every aspect of the journey all at once. Break it up into one baby step at a time. You go to Point B, then to C, then to D, and so on.
17. For this trip only: Don't be such a perfectionist. Whatever happens, "Let it happen." Make up your mind to enjoy it all.
18. And, perhaps the most important point of all: Act *as if* you're already cured.

CHAPTER 13

Anticipatory Anxiety

"If I'm not nervous before a show, I know I'm not going to be at my best that night."

—*Jack Benny*

Sometimes a state of "anticipatory anxiety," or excitement, is deliberately sought. Think of the Indian war dances before a battle. Or the African jungle drums before a hunt. All this is an attempt to rev up the system physically and get the warriors ready.

But the way some people talk (with dread) about anticipatory anxiety, you'd think it was the name of a new disease!

Whenever *anyone* faces an important event—for you, it may be going to the supermarket; for someone else, it may be giving a lecture or looking for a job—there's bound to be a higher level of brain activity and neural excitation than if one is relaxing in an armchair.

Some excited anticipation before an important event is entirely normal, especially when a person believes that the particular act he is about to perform will have an effect on his whole future. Even seasoned actors and actresses experience some butterflies before a performance.

There's certainly nothing unusual about that. These people are putting themselves on the line. The acts they'll soon be performing are important to them. So the nervous system has to build up momentum for a good performance. It only becomes a problem when you worry about it too much.

I (SSJ) was once watching a race on TV and the camera zoomed in on the runners. I could actually see the muscle tension in the legs as the runners crouched in position, waiting for the race to begin. Their muscles were quivering. But once that shot was fired, all their tremendous pent-up energy was suddenly released. It's like a coiled-up spring that's suddenly let go. The analogy is apt because muscle fibers (if you were to view them under a microscope) actually coil up and shorten when they're held in a state of anticipation. That's to prepare the body for action. But once the action is taken, the tension diminishes. The muscle fibers lengthen and become stretched out again.

If you own a cat, watch him the next time he's preparing to attack. His whole body fairly ripples from the strain. Those muscles he'll be using are coiling up, shortening, getting wound up for the leap.

But is the runner concerned or worried because his muscles quiver before a race? Is your cat concerned because his tail twitches? No, of course not. They're not observing themselves. Their minds are focused only on the activity they intend to perform. Notice I didn't say "about to perform" but "intend to perform." In other words, they are doing this willingly and with purpose. They're not adding more tension by observing themselves and berating themselves because they're nervous.

But what can you do if your nervous system is a bit too revved up for comfort?

You can always tone it down by changing your perception of the situation. You can minimize its importance. You can pretend (or really believe, if you can) that the event about to take place is not as earth-shattering as it seems, that in the long run it's of little significance in your life. You can lessen the importance of the event by *choosing* to see it this way. You can remind yourself that in the cosmic scheme of things, this particular event ranks pretty low, that it's no big deal. (It's the old "sour grapes" mechanism.)

This self-dialogue will effectively take the edge off the panic. Why? Because if you tell yourself there's no race, nothing worth fighting for, then there's no point in getting all revved up, is there?

When I (SS) did my first radio interview on panic attacks, I was quite nervous. I went to the studio by subway, and as I sat in the train looking around at the people there, I thought, "Hmm-m. These are just ordinary people, like me. It's no big deal, really. And even if I say something stupid—so what? These people look like they couldn't care less . . ." I calmed down and by the time I walked into the studio, I felt confident and joyful. Before we went on the air, the interviewer surprised me by saying, "Don't worry—we've arranged to play some interlude music if you should get a panic attack while talking." I laughed. "That won't be necessary," I said.

So you have two very useful tools to work with: First, to realize that your nervous system is just behaving normally when it gets excited before an important event. And second, to know that you can lower your excitement at will by changing your perception of the situation.

Take Your Time

Many panic attack sufferers are very impatient. They want to get more and more done before some (often imaginary) deadline. They want to rush time, speed the river along, faster, faster. If they're out, they're always looking at the clock, counting the minutes till they can leave and run back home. When they're home, they want to be instantly cured— so they can rush out again. No wonder Dr. Weekes has, as one of her basic principles, the admonition to "let time pass."

I (SS) remember once, long ago, being on a bus in Manhattan. I was already late for an appointment and the bus was stuck in heavy traffic. Cars and taxis were honking their horns; there was confusion all around; and my bus was not moving. I was very impatient. I wanted the bus to go—*now*. I clearly remember looking down at my hands. I had grabbed the seat in front of me and was straining to "push" the bus from the inside! At least I had the wits to realize what I was doing, and I stopped. Now, whenever I find myself in any vehicle (or in any situation beyond my control), I simply relax and let the driver take over. I don't "assist" anymore.

What can you do to counteract this rush-rush tendency? First of all, and this is an obvious first step, you have to allow plenty of time to prepare things so you don't have to rush. (For instance, in the example I gave above, I could have left the house much earlier.)

Secondly, there's the temptation to do everything at once. So you just have to repeat to yourself firmly, "I'll only do one thing at a time." And do it that way.

Another very effective measure is this: Stop where you are and begin to do everything in s-l-o-w motion. Many people have a bad habit of rushing around the house just before they leave, checking to see if they left the gas on, looking for their keys, or their sweater. So all you do is switch to slow motion. If you consistently move with an exaggerated slow action, that will soon become a signal to you, an automatic response, to slow down.

Here's what one of our clients told us:

Every morning, my son has to be in school by 12:30. So you'd think I had plenty of time to get ready and I wouldn't have to rush. But I always used to be what I'd call a last minute person. As the time would draw near when I had to take my son to school, I'd start rushing around the house like a maniac, looking for my key, looking for his jacket, and I'd get to school all tense and jittery.

But now it's so different—since my counselor told me about this slow-motion technique. I just go around and do what I have to do—but slowly. Everything gets done. I don't feel rushed. My son is on time. And when I get to school I'm calm and I talk with the other mothers. That rush-rush feeling is gone, and my days are a lot easier now!

Those Constant What-ifs

Constant what-iffing seems to be the trademark of the panic attack sufferer.

And yet such thinking isn't bad—by itself. After all, all our inventions, our great ideas in the arts, in the sciences, must have started with this one basic question: "What if it works like this . . . ?" Or: "What if I do this differently . . . ?" That's what Edison did, didn't he? He must have asked himself thousands of times: "What if I use this material as a filament instead of that?" And then there was light! (Can you just picture Colonel Sanders asking himself, "What if ah make up a batch of Mother's chicken recipe and sell it?" Or Picasso asking himself, "Hm-m. What if I paint three eyes instead of two?")

So, what-if questions and looking ahead can be tremendously useful and appropriate—in their place. But if all your questions are: "What if I go there and get into an accident?" "What if I didn't shut off the gas and the house explodes?" or: "What if I go there and get a panic attack?"—you've simply placed all your creative energy into one basket—and the wrong basket, at that!

You have a questioning, think-ahead mind. You're evidently creative. Many people we've known through our program write poetry, or books. They paint, do needlework, or woodwork. We are seeing, I think, a far greater percentage of artistic people than could be accounted for on a statistical basis. But you have taken these wonderful, God-given gifts—

and put them to wrong use. You've been creating colorful pictures of catastrophes wherever you go. It's time you took your creative imagination and turned it around—and let it work *for* you instead of against you!

Answering Those What-ifs

Never be afraid to face your what-ifs, and to answer them in kind.

Some people, in an attempt to rid themselves of the constantly tormenting question "What if?", make the mistake of trying to turn off all such thoughts by refusing to think about them. Whenever such a thought comes sneaking around, they become alarmed and do their best to squelch that thought—without even examining it. (Some even wear a rubber band tied to their wrist, so they can snap it—and punish themselves—whenever a what-if thought comes along!)

But this method is self-defeating. It only makes the thought cling to you more and more. You always have to feel free to look at your own thoughts and feelings—no matter what they are. This is not to say, of course, that you should constantly analyze your thoughts—or take your mental temperature all the time, so to speak. ("Now, what am I feeling right now?"; "What do I feel like doing?") Being overly concerned about transient moods or paying too much attention to fleeting emotions is not such a great idea, either. But when a serious what-if question comes to your mind, you don't have to be afraid to examine it and answer it.

A few examples come to mind: An out-of-town guest and I (SS) were traveling by subway. At one point, the subway became an elevated line and as we looked out the window, my friend noted a curve ahead, on the line. She started to get very worried for fear the train wouldn't make the curve. She had never been on an elevated before, and the thought—naturally enough—occurred to her: "What if the

train falls down?" I reassured her by telling her that this elevated line was built long before I was born and that this very
train and other trains like it had been making daily trips for
many, many years without mishap. Therefore, the chance of
the train falling down within the next few minutes was very,
very remote indeed. She immediately became calm again.

One client, who used the subway to go to work, became
fearful whenever the train stopped between stations; most of
his panic attacks would occur during those times. At some
level, he was seeing the halted train as a sign of great danger.
("Uh-oh, now there's trouble—something must have happened.") So, of course, his sentry reacted—why shouldn't it?
But after we talked about it, he began to see the situation
more realistically.

I pointed out that there are traffic signals in a subway tunnel, just as there are in the streets. (Of course, he knew this;
it just didn't register at the time.) When there is a train just
ahead, I said, your train has to stop in order to avoid a collision. The motorman must obey the signals and stop as a
safety measure. Now the halted train became associated with
safety rather than with danger. I also suggested to my client
that he look around him and watch the other passengers
during one of these train stops. I've been riding the subways
for years and have always observed how nervous people get
whenever the train stops between stations—especially if it's a
long stop. People start to cough, to fidget, to look around
with worried expressions. They're literally left in the dark.
(In fact, so many people complained about this problem
that the transit authority finally installed speakers in the cars
so the motormen could announce, during stops, the reason
for the halt and, if necessary, give instructions.) I was able to
convince this man that he wasn't the only one; that there was
no shame about being afraid or uneasy.

So, you see, a realistic appraisal of the situation can be as
important a tool as fantasy. As this man began to view the situation in a different light, he was able to turn the situation

around. The panic attacks in the train subsided and he was now able to ride the subway quite comfortably, without becoming unduly alarmed about a halted train.

Another instance: a former client was traveling by car along an unfamiliar mountain road at night. He was alone. At one point he felt very tense and uncomfortable. But he used a relaxation technique and the moment passed. Later, however, he was quite disturbed by what he imagined was a return of the panic attacks that he used to experience. Evidently, this what-if thought must have crossed his mind as he drove: "What if my car tumbles over the cliff?" It's a natural thought that any driver might have. By being aware of the danger, one drives more carefully. (That's the purpose of fear, isn't it?) So, instead of trying to silence that thought, he might have answered it: "Look, I'm a good driver—and I'm careful. I'm not going too fast. And I've traveled unfamiliar roads before—and I got through all right. So I'm pretty safe."

The only way you can dispel those bad what-ifs is by confronting them—and answering them. How do you answer them? That depends on the situation. Most of them can be dismissed by just putting the word "so" in front of the sentence you tell yourself: "So what if I go there and get a panic attack?" (Big, hairy deal . . . !) Others require logic and reason (as in the abovementioned illustrations).

Here are some other useful counterquestions: "What are the chances of such-and-such happening?" Or: "What is the worst that can possibly happen?"

And sometimes you just have to say to yourself: "I'm going to face that with courage."

The Fear of Being Nervous

Many people get so upset when they become nervous. I think that, as human beings, we're entitled to be nervous on occasion—without making a federal case out of it. Years ago, there was a character in the Dick Tracy comic strip called Fearless Fosdick. He "didn't have a nerve in his body." But he was a made-up character. Real flesh-and-blood people are nervous sometimes. And they do feel frightened at times. But—so what? A little excitement now and then never hurt anyone.

Once you admit that it's OK to be nervous (especially when there's something to be nervous about!), the paradox, of course, is that this admission usually reduces the level of nervousness.

And you can do another thing: As we pointed out before, you can convert your nervousness into enthusiasm—and enjoy the excitement of being aware and alive.

A certain story comes to mind. I (SS) remember one of my clients, a young man of twenty, who had suffered from agoraphobia for several years and had been homebound for several months when he started this program. Once he was able to go out again, naturally enough, he wanted to start dating. He knew he'd be nervous on his first date, and he was afraid that his nervousness would turn into panic attacks again. I advised him to convert that excess nervous energy into enthusiasm—for his date. To focus all his attention on her, not on himself—and to make her feel she was the "prettiest girl in the world."

Well, it worked like a charm. I understand he became immensely popular with the girls by applying this method. (The fact that he also happened to be tall, dark, and handsome didn't hurt any either.)

By the way, there's a rather novel twist to this story: About six months later, he called me again, just to say hello. It seems he found a job in Manhattan and was living it up in an apartment he shared with friends in Greenwich Village. He told me there was lots of partying going on—often the parties lasted till dawn—and that he wasn't exactly following his diet any more. The panic attacks were coming back, he said.

"But," he added, "I've never had so much fun in my life! If panic attacks are the price I have to pay, well, that's it, then. I'll pay."

I told him, "Listen—who am I to quarrel with you? If it's OK with you, it's certainly OK with me." He felt in control, you see. He knew what they were; he knew what would make them go away—*if* he chose to do so. And he wasn't worried about them.

Watching Your Self

The mind is meant to be used as an instrument to examine the outside world, to reflect, perhaps, on the inner world, in a philosophical sense, and to somehow bring them together in harmony. The mind was not designed for constant introspection, perpetual self-analysis, endless self-absorption. If you do this, you're not using your body/mind correctly—the way nature intended. Just as a stomach is not supposed to digest itself, only what's put into it—so a mind has to be directed "out there" and not always inwardly, watching your Self all the time.

If you know someone is watching you all the time, doesn't that make you a little uneasy? Being observed by anybody—including your own Self—can make a person so self-conscious that it would be hard to do anything right. Try this: Walk across a room and be aware each second of how you move your arms, how you bend your right knee, how you bend your left knee, and so on. A person watching you walk like that would think you're a wooden soldier. Being so self-conscious (which, literally, means conscious of your Self) tends to jam the machinery. Your body can't operate smoothly.

There's a little anecdote about a mediocre tennis player who always beat his opponents, who were much better players. Someone asked him, "How in the world did you ever manage to beat so-and-so?" He replied, "Simple. All I did was ask him: 'Do you take a breath before or after you serve?'"

When you go out, you're not supposed to be thinking about how your legs move, how you're feeling, whether you're breathing the right way—or things like that. This intense concentration with your Self can only bring on the very thing you *don't* want to happen.

So, when you go somewhere—switch to automatic; let your mind wander on the other matters (ideas, letter-writing, thinking things out, whatever). In other words, *"you"* get out of the way.

CHAPTER 14

Dealing with the Unknown

"On this subject, my adopted mottos are: 'Don't worry until you have to,' and 'One door closes, another door opens.'
—*Shirley Swede*

Many people have the mistaken notion that being cured means going out into the world willy-nilly, wandering about here and there without feeling anything but a carefree state of freedom. What a lot of cat-fat! I don't know why this vagabond myth is so widespread, but it is.

To many people who suffer from panic attacks, there seems to be a wide chasm between the sick and the well. But it really isn't so. What normal person just picks himself up and hops on a train (or plane) and heads for who knows where? Do you know anyone who says to himself, "Hm, let's see . . . today's Sunday. I think I'll take a flight down to Pickleville, Arkansas—just to see what it's like"? Do you know anyone like that? (Neither do I.) Everyone is more comfortable with the known, the familiar—and somewhat leery of the unknown. That's just how the human organism is wired.

You can observe this all around you. At a meeting, for instance, nine times out of ten, people will choose the same chair they had the last time. We all have our little daily habits related to dressing, eating, sleeping. Change is difficult for everyone—but, naturally, in varying degrees. Even those who, by any standards, are considered hardy and adventurous still have the same need for the familiar, the known. Columbus knew where he was going. Or thought he knew. I'm sure he plotted and charted his journey on the maps of his day. The explorers who went to the Poles knew where they were going; they made provisions against the cold—and learned whatever was knowable about the regions they were going into.

Watch a small child beginning to explore his environment. He stands on his little two feet, takes a few steps forward, pokes little fingers at something strange on the table, tests the table by touching it, slapping it, then looks back to Mama for approval. If she nods and smiles, the baby goes on with his exploring—testing, taking little steps, always coming back to safe ground, then trying again. And this pattern is repeated throughout life: looking ahead, trying to understand, to conquer the unknown little by little; testing it, bringing it slowly into the known world. Nobody rides off into the unknown without a plan or purpose.

I remember when I (SS) embarked on a program to unmask the unknown. I went to visit Kennedy Airport in preparation for my "maiden voyage": a trip to Holland. I talked to people waiting on line for tickets . . . passengers who had just arrived . . . porters standing at the curb . . . anyone I could grab hold of. Most people told me—yes, they, too, were afraid to fly the first time. But now, after having flown several times, for them it was "like sitting in my living room." I went to the observation deck and watched for hours, planes taking off and landing. (The grace of those huge metal birds was unbelievable!)

Not only did I go to the airport, but I read as much as I could about the history of aviation and the principles of aerodynamics. When the day finally came and I walked into that plane, I *acted as if* I were a seasoned traveler. There were many babies on that plane. I pretended (inside myself) that I was a baby, too—being taken by my mommy on the plane.

The trip itself was fantastic! (All that homework paid off.) I watched the sun come up at 3 A.M. by my watch. I looked down and, mirrorlike, saw pink-and-blue clouds. I thought: How many men in countless ages must have yearned to fly. I remember reading a story about the Greek who ordered huge wings to be fashioned out of eagle feathers, but the heat of the sun melted the wax that held them together. And here I was, I thought, privileged to do what kings and princes were unable to do in ages past. Such were the musings that occupied my thoughts. And that was what turned the trip into the enjoyable experience that it was. Had I directed my thoughts to plane crashes and skyjacking—well, you can imagine how that would have worked out!

So it's your job to find out all you can about where you want to go. It's your job to bring the unknown into the realm of the known.

It doesn't make sense to consider yourself abnormal and berate yourself because you crave the familiar. With the right mind-set, however, you can learn to venture out.

Switching Bases

When I (SS) was visiting in Texas, I thought of the house I was staying at—not my house in New York—as my home base. Wherever you go, you can create a temporary home base. If you're traveling by bus (sightseeing on an extended trip), let that bus become your home base. If you're traveling by car, let the car become your home base. If you're staying at a hotel, that becomes your home base—and so on.

People who travel a lot become very adept at switching bases. When they go to another city, they frequently check in at the same hotel chain. It's probably no mere coincidence that chain hotel rooms look the same. Yes, there's the financial aspect; it's cheaper when management can buy in quantity. But I think another reason is that management knows people are more comfortable in familiar surroundings. You can go all over the world and check into any chain hotel and, except for some local variations and color, you get pretty much the same accommodations.

Have you ever watched a square dance? There's one part where the partners dance in a circle in opposite directions, passing from one person to another until they're back in the same place. As they let go of one person's hand, they immediately reach for another person's hand—and so on. So they are always holding someone's hand as they move along. Well, traveling is pretty much like that, too. You let go of one place—and you immediately start thinking of another. You say good-bye to your friends at one airport—you greet other friends at another airport.

The only thing is that you have to become more skillful, more agile, at switching bases. As soon as you let go of one home base, you latch onto another. It doesn't have to be an actual, physical base. That's not important. It should be more a matter of mind. When people go somewhere, they usually happily anticipate being in the new place (seeing new surroundings, meeting people). They've already starting to think of the place they're going to as their new base of operations.

Free as a Bird

Dr. Desmond Morris suggests that the fear of being alone in a wide open space may have been programmed in the human brain as a protective mechanism. This goes back in our ancestry, many thousands of years ago, when we lived as members of a hunting tribe. Being alone in a field, or anywhere away from the tribe, would have meant certain danger. Thus, fear of leaving the tribe (with its relative safety) had survival value, and this trait was passed on to the next generation. So perhaps even today this ancient inborn fear is still with us.

Yet I (SSJ) always thought the expression "free as a bird" was an apt one; after all, can't a bird fly wherever it wants to—without restriction? But I discovered that's not so, that birds are also confined to certain boundaries just as animals and people are.

I recently read a story about birds (*Reader's Digest*, "Birds Live in Nature's Invisible Cage," by John and Jean George) that may be astonishing to the non-bird-watcher. Bird behavior, the authors tell us, "is so rigidly fixed that birds are . . . slaves to the air they fly through." One of the examples they gave was that of a cardinal whose home base had just been stripped of trees by bulldozers to make way for a new development. "As we watched," they wrote, "the bird flew about 400 feet, then suddenly back-winged as if he had hit an invisible wall. After flapping to earth, he flew off in another direction, only to smash into another invisible barrier." The boundaries of its territory were so firmly fixed in its mind that it was literally unable to fly across the clearing to safety. There were predator screech owls in the adjacent woods, and, just as they predicted, the authors found their cardinal's bloodstained feathers the following morning.

Territorial instincts are strongest in birds. Their forebrains are not well developed, so they rely more on instincts in order to survive. (The territorial instinct helps to establish and maintain pair formation, thus aiding the survival of the species.) Of course, we humans also operate by instinct in many ways. But in our species, the role of instinct is attenuated; it doesn't play such an important role in regulating behavior. We can rely on our large thinking brain. We can reason, we can question, and we can make creative use of imagery. As human beings, we have the capacity to see a situation in a new light. We also have the ability to *redefine* a situation and read new meanings into it.

So, make the most of your thinking cortex! Instead of narrowly outlining a certain territory and saying, "This is *my* specific area (*my* block, *my* neighborhood, *my* house, etc.)," you can mentally enlarge that same territory to encompass a much wider space. "This whole city or this whole country or this whole world is 'mine.' I'm still in 'my' safe place; I belong here."

The unfortunate bird was unable to redefine its area. He couldn't see the overall situation and judge it from a different perspective. All he could do was obey and give in to the instinct he was programmed for.

But *you're* in a position to do otherwise!

CHAPTER 15

Gaining Confidence by Doing

"Build with the rocks you stumble over."
—*The Christophers*

The curious thing about panic attacks is that they soon begin to take on a life of their own. You think about them as you go about your daily activities; you worry about them; you read avidly about them; you talk to doctors about them. After a while, the panic attacks become an important part of your life. The minute you open your eyes in the morning, "It" is there—with a capital I!

That's why we're always telling our clients how important it is to get interested—*really* interested—in something other than panic attacks. Something that brings you in contact with other people. Perhaps a little business of your own, a club, a Bible study group, or volunteer work. You know, of course, that the mind can only think of one thing at a time; if you have a growing interest in whatever it may be, that interest, by its very presence in your life, will push away the constant grim reminder of panic attacks. But if you lie around the house staring into space (asking over and over again, "Why me?"), or watching one foolish TV show after another, how can you expect your life to change?

All any therapy can do is help you to help yourself. Even if you go to a therapist, all he can do is point you in the right direction so that your body/mind can heal itself. The therapist can't think for you. He only helps you gain new insights that enable you to tackle your problems in a different way. Sure, this book can help; other books can help. But you have to sift through all this (and other) information, and put to work those suggestions that seem reasonable and right to you. If one thing doesn't work, try another. It's your willingness to apply this information that will ultimately change things and make the situation better.

So the bottom line is this: *You* have to want to get well; *you* have to do the things that will get you well. Nobody else can do them for you.

As someone once said, "Part of the cure is to wish to be cured."

Developing a Real Interest

A number of phobia organizations and clinics are teaching the following method as a means of controlling panic. When a panic attack comes on or when you become anxious (so this system teaches), you're supposed to immediately measure the level of anxiety you're at—and rate it on a scale from one to ten. (One is the lowest, ten the highest.) Then, you're supposed to watch your level of anxiety go up or down. ("I'm at a five now; now it's going up to an eight; now it's going down to a six," and so on.) It is hoped that playing this numbers game will somehow disrupt the rising barometer of panic and make it come down again.

This method not only strikes us as a bit too contrived, but, most important, we really question its effectiveness. (Maybe it does work for some, but, of course, we've been seeing people for whom this method hasn't worked.) The main reason we disapprove of this method is because it rivets attention on the Self; on the moment of panic; on the physical symptoms. And, as we pointed out, one of the things that causes the panic attacks to come in the first place is this habit of introspection, of focusing too much on the Self. Sufferers of panic attacks, as we mentioned earlier, tend to question all the time, "How am I feeling? What does this symptom mean?" It's this caring so much how one is feeling every single minute—and the unwillingness to tolerate any uncomfortable moments—that are at the heart of this problem.

In addition to the counting and rating oneself on a scale from one to ten, you're also supposed to, according to the method, concentrate on the here and now—by looking at trees, watching cars pass, for example. But again, we think this method is counterproductive *if* it's done in a frenzied attempt to stave off the panic attack. If the person's self-talk is something like this: "Quick—I must distract myself—look at the tree, look at the tree, concentrate on the tree!" This is not to say that one cannot use this method in a much better way. I've done this many times myself. The better way would be to really stop and *look* at the trees . . . the flowers . . . to take delight in their beauty.

Sometimes, when I have several important errands to do and I catch myself walking too fast, rushing around, I deliberately slow down, stop, and really look at my surroundings with the intent to enjoy. I might stop to admire the delicate colors of a rose in somebody's garden. Or look up at the sunset and enjoy the riot of colors I see and try to imagine how I would paint it. This pause for beauty refreshes me and it gives me a new perspective on life. (I think: "This errand I'm rushing to do—is it really so important from a cosmic view? Will anyone care a year from now? Will I? So what if I don't get it all done today . . . there's always tomorrow. Let me enjoy today, let me see the beauty now, while I can.")

You cannot refresh your nervous system if you're frantically searching for something, anything, in a grasping way—in an attempt to divert your attention. On the contrary, it will tend to do the opposite—it will make you more nervous. Why? Because you just know normal people don't go around saying, in desperation, "Look at the tree, look at the tree." So, part of your mind (that stern Self that's always looking at you with such a critical eye) starts to mumble, "Tsk . . . tsk . . . tsk. . . . There's something not-quite-right here!" And this thought scares you all over again.

When you're walking down the street, half thinking of a panic attack, it's a little bit late to be acquiring a burning interest in something else. This has to be done long before. You have to prepare your mind. Ideas just don't grow out of the air. You have to have some input—and then, out of that, you gradually develop new interests. Something strikes your fancy; something touches off a new concept. Then you follow your own bent and guide these budding ideas into new channels. Here are a few examples from my (SS) own experiences.

Some years ago, I worked at a hospital. There I met a group of French-speaking employees with whom I became quite friendly. We often had lunch together. That prompted me to renew my study of high school French. Every day, I would write down vocabulary on index cards and I would memorize the words as I walked or waited for the train or the elevator. (Index cards are easy to carry in your hand or your pocket.) My goal was to memorize thirty words a day. I'd forget twenty—but even so, I made progress. My pleasure at my increased fluency in the language prompted me to study with even greater zeal. And that's how interests grow: through pleasurable feedback.

At another time in my life, I used to write poetry. Constantly. I'd carry a little notebook with me—and I'd be scribbling away on the train, every day on my way to work. It kept me so occupied. I'd often look up in astonishment: "What? Is this my station—already?"

While I (SSJ) was attending medical school, I took a part-time job. I purposely took a job that was so boring and uninspiring that my mind would be freed to study and think. I also wrote out my lessons and study material on index cards, and I'd memorize this information during the day, as I went along doing repetitive tasks.

You, too, can choose an area of study—something you always wanted to do but never found the time to do before. Well, now is the time. Not only will you become an "expert" on your favorite topic, but you'll also be so busy you won't have time to worry about panic attacks.

So doesn't it make more sense to develop a real interest in something—and use that as a focal point—rather than counting the cracks in the sidewalk?

Do You See How Far You Can Go?

Some phobia organizations teach the following: See how far you can go without panicking—and then, if you panic, turn back, go home, and try again another day.

But that's exactly what you've been doing! And, as you've discovered, that doesn't work at all. And why should it? Even if you're feeling all right at the moment, can you predict how you'll feel twenty minutes from now? So, if you go too far and "it" happens (this mind-set tells you), how will you get back in time to your "safe place"? This viewpoint discourages you from ever going too far from home.

We asked several clients what they thought of this method of "seeing how far you can go" and this is what they said.

"If you allow yourself to run from a situation once you're in it, it can become a crutch. You never really train yourself to relax and get through it. In order to 'desensitize' yourself, it's important to follow through once you've started."

"I feel that once you turn back, you're apt to have many negative feelings—about yourself, about recovery, and so on. This program stresses the need to proceed onward and not to turn back. And this has worked for me. There have been times when I wanted to turn back, but I didn't. Each time, after I followed through, I felt such a sense of accomplishment. It was rewarding to see that I could rise above those negative thoughts."

"I disagree with that approach because I know from experience that it doesn't work. It can easily turn into a continuing pattern of escaping. I think that you can only make progress when there is positive learning— and a growing sense of control over your own actions. In fact, it seems to me that this approach would only add to feelings of discouragement and make the next time even more frightening."

"In my experience, when I turned back, the whole negative experience was only magnified the next time I tried. It's far better to develop useful skills for helping you go a step further, rather than turning around and escaping."

The Moment of Truth

Suppose you start to do something or go somewhere and you're suddenly hit with the realization: "I can't back out now!" What do you do when you arrive at that point of no return? How do you handle it?

This is the moment to try all your relaxation techniques: To start breathing slowly. To drop those muscles to the floor and let gravity pull at them. To do the QR or the First Aid. There may be a powerful physical need to hyperventilate. (After all, you've already aroused your sentry by that thought: "Well, this is it . . . there's no turning back now . . . I must go through with it, come hell or high water!")

So that's pretty scary. That's when that timid, dependent

child in you cries, "Ooh, I can't stand it!!" But just speak firmly to that child. Not harshly, but firmly. Say things like: "C'mon, honey, that's OK." Or: "C'mon, let's show 'em the stuff you're made of . . ." As each moment passes, and you find you haven't disintegrated yet, remind yourself of this fact. Keep on reminding yourself. Tell yourself how fine you're doing, under the circumstances. (Talk nicely: Remember, you're talking to a small, frightened child.) Never mind that you're quaking in your boots; that's not the point. The point is you are already in a situation, you're finally doing it (whatever "it" is for you). You've taken action. So congratulate yourself for this. Be proud. This is cause for celebration, not censure. The nervousness—don't worry about it. It'll subside later on, after you get more experienced in whatever it is you're doing.

I (SS) remember when I was learning to drive—and the first time I drove on the highway. Was I scared? You bet! I was with my husband—and as I slid over to take the wheel, I reviewed in my mind all my strong points: I'd done very well driving in the streets. I'd already gone up and down hills—even steep hills. I'm a careful, sane driver. My husband had confidence in my driving ability. (If he could turn over his precious car to me, I must really be doing great!) I simply ignored the feelings of fear because I knew those feelings weren't particularly significant. Anybody doing something like this for the first time would be nervous. (Sure, I knew there were hotshot boys who wouldn't be afraid to drive on the highway—but they weren't me.)

So, instead of berating myself for not being cool—or wishing I wasn't there—I concentrated on what I was doing and on relaxing myself. (I did the slow abdominal breathing; I made my body heavy, and so on.) And as I drove along, I began to enjoy the scenery, which was so beautiful (we were in the Catskill Mountain region). Afterward, when it was over, I felt as exhilarated as if I'd just won a prize! Sentences like this were dancing in my head: "Wow, I did it—I really did it!" "I'm a driver now." "It was a lot easier than I thought!" "I'm brave, I can do it, I've got what it takes," and so on.

This is how confidence is built—slowly, bit by bit. Confidence doesn't come from reading a book on it or by programming yourself: "I *will* have confidence, I *will* have confidence." Confidence comes by *doing*.

So don't wait for confidence to come knocking at your door before you start doing. That's putting it all backward. Your confidence will build naturally with each task you accomplish, each time you're able to say, "Hooray, I did it!"

That Safe Person

You really don't need a safe person. You *are* that safe person. Think of it: Everything you need you already have. It's all inside of you. We are, each of us, whole and sufficient for what we have to do. The hope, the courage, the life force, if you will—are inside us. And we can call on this source of strength whenever we want to.

Even what we call outside sources of strength are still inside of us—in our own minds. The books you've read, the people you know, the people you love, the God you believe in—aren't all these things an intricate part of your Self?

An old legend tells that when Man was first made, all the angels were jealous because Man was given courage derived from the Divine Spark itself. So the angels conspired to hide this knowledge from Man, and they looked around for a hiding place. One angel said, "Let's hide it in the sky." Another said, "Let's put it into the earth." Still another said, "Let's throw it into the water." But one wise angel said, "No, let's hide it in the heart of Man himself. He'll never think of looking there!"

You're OK!

Sometimes it's hard to convince a person that he's normal, that his nervous system is functioning just fine. Despite rational explanations, some people for some reason want to hold on to the belief that they're sick. Many psychologists slyly suggest there is a manipulative factor at work here. Yet Dr. Weekes writes in *Simple Effective Treatment of Agoraphobia,* "I have rarely met the agoraphobic man or woman who has no wish to recover."

Maybe there is some validity in both points of view. At any rate, with some people there's a recurrent, underlying phrase that runs like a leitmotif throughout their thoughts: "Something is wrong with me"—despite evidence to the contrary.

For example, I (SS) once had a client who could only function well within a certain boundary—a ten-block radius from his house. As soon as he left his area, he would promptly get a panic attack. One day, about two weeks after he joined the program, a friend of his passed away, and he felt he had to visit the family to pay his respects. The only trouble was that the house was some distance away, out of his "boundary." But he drove there anyhow.

On the way home, even before he got into his car, he was overwhelmed by panic. He described to me his "wild ride" home—passing buses and cars and scooting in and out of traffic. It was only when his car finally screeched to a halt in front of his house that he could let go and relax. He therefore knew there was something inherently wrong with his nervous system.

"Look," I pointed out to him, "you were driving in heavy rush-hour traffic. On the way home, you must have passed hundreds and hundreds, if not thousands, of cars. Throughout all that crazy New York traffic, you were maneuvering your car successfully. Your nervous system was able to respond accurately to the thousands of clues bombarding your senses.

With all that, you arrived home safely. And you want to tell me something is wrong with your nervous system?"

I never found out what subsequently became of this client. He quit the program the following week.

The Urge to Run Away

When you experience a panic attack (or when you feel one is imminent), you get a strong, unmistakable urge to run away. It has little to do with any voluntary desire; it's an automatic response that occurs whenever the sentry is aroused. In fact, whenever you get the urge to run away, that's a pretty sure sign that your fight-or-flight instinct is activated. (That's what the phrase describes, doesn't it?)

But please note: The urge to run away when the hypothalamus is aroused is *not* abnormal. That's how the body was designed: During a time of danger, nature wants to help you get out of the way.

But if you *know* there's no danger, if you know it's just your own nervous overreaction, do *not* give in to the urge to run away. What should you do instead? Immediately go into the QR. Or the First Aid Treatment. Once the sentry quiets down the urge to run disappears.

If you give in to the urge to run, later you will feel defeated and angry at yourself. Whereas if you don't run away but calm yourself instead, later you will feel a triumphant sense of victory. (Which would you rather have— the short-term or the long-term gain?)

Remember, as you continue to follow this program, the sympathetic nervous system will calm down. And as it calms down, your habitual overreaction diminishes.

Here's a letter in our files from one of our former clients:

I'm feeling stronger from the improved diet and exercise in following the program, so I decided to take an evening walk to a nearby movie theater and see a film. I packed some cottage cheese, whole wheat crackers, raisins, and a nectarine and set off into the night, aware of the "anticipatory anxiety" about going to a long movie alone, but determined to relax through any "episodes" that might arrive during the night. There were several mild rev-ups, but instead of bolting out of the theater, I kept reminding myself of everything I learned from the PASS program and from Dr. Weekes's book, and repeated the QR and kept catching myself tensing my muscles and coaching myself to relax them—to "let go"—and telling myself I was physically OK: that the worst that could happen would be I would scare myself into being very uncomfortable and also that I could choose *not* to do so.

After a while and after eating, things cleared up and my walk back home late at night (which I had also been concerned about earlier) was absolutely jubilant because of doing the right things and practicing the right attitude. I know it may sound simple and corny, but it was really quite a *triumph!* I learned how wonderful and enjoyable something can become if you don't view it as a dreadful task, and if you keep reminding yourself that you're really healthy.

This young man—believe it or not—eventually became a world traveler. He told me he goes on "trains, planes, everything—without batting an eyelash!"

Feeling Trapped

One of the characteristics of agoraphobia is that the person is constantly seeing himself, in almost any situation he finds himself in, as the victim—the "trappee," to coin a word. Take, for example, the woman who is afraid of crossing a bridge, especially in heavy traffic. If you ask her why she's afraid, she explains she's afraid of "being trapped there," of not being able to escape when those feelings come over her.

In order to conquer this fear, certain changes have to be made to diminish the physical overreaction to the situation, and to alter her *perception* of the situation. In other words, both body and mind have to be considered.

For example, she has to make sure she's not getting run-down again. She should be eating right and do daily exercise and relaxation. She should bring food along for the trip, remembering that stress uses up a lot of energy. She should also be armed with stress-reducing tools. All these things are just commonsense precautions.

It would also be helpful to learn more about bridges— how they're constructed, their history, etc. This information might seem to be irrelevant, but it's really not. Whatever becomes more familiar, more comprehensible, also becomes less threatening.

It's also essential that she begin to see the situation from a different perspective. After all, she's not on the bridge simply by chance. She's either going somewhere or she's coming home. The bridge is there for a reason, too; there's an obstacle—a river, a highway—and the bridge was built in order to make it easier (or possible) for people to cross to the other side. So she's using the bridge in order to get to where she's going; the bridge isn't using her! In other words, she's not a helpless victim who happens to be caught on a bridge. She's there for a reason.

If you keep seeing the fear only as an outside force that you have nothing to do with, then you're only delaying your own recovery. Even if you're taking medication, you still have to be responsible for the way you eat, think, manage stress, etc. A pill isn't the answer. It's just one of those paradoxes: Once you see this problem as something you yourself have a lot to do with, you'll have a much better handle on it.

I (SS) remember reading a story in the newspaper a few

years ago about a group of mountain climbers who were trapped in a cave when a landslide occurred. They were all eventually rescued. But it's interesting to note that the leader warned the group to lie quietly in order to conserve oxygen. Why? because relaxed muscles don't need as much oxygen.

But what do *you* do when you feel trapped? You immediately tense all your muscles (using up oxygen and making more lactic acid) as you frantically look for an exit. If you keep on saying to yourself, "I'm trapped," it's like waving a red flag in front of a bull. Because "I'm trapped" means to prepare the body to flee. Words are important. They're the symbols that pave the way for our thoughts to follow.

So use calming, comforting words. Change your viewpoint. Throw away that victim mentality; see yourself as brave. See yourself as a *user* of modern technology (bridges, cars, trains, etc.). These inventions provide important services, and they enable us to get to where we want to go.

The Escape Hatch

I (SS) remember reading about an ancient battle involving an invasion. The invading army arrived in ships, and after they landed, the commander ordered all the ships to be burned.

Many people go into a situation anticipating retreat— even before they get there. They are armed with knowledge, but they don't really intend to use it; their thoughts are already focused on the escape hatch. (Dr. Weekes says that people will go 99 percent of the way but are unwilling to go that extra 1 percent that will bring them victory.)

But you can't have this attitude and expect at the same time to be calm and serene. Why? Because that mind-set brings still more tension to the situation. Instead of quieting you, it presents you with yet another tension-provoking option and more questions: How will I get out of it? What will I say? How will I explain this to my friends? What'll they think of me? Will they know my secret? And how can I explain this to myself? Am I really a coward at heart?

So this is the key: Go into a situation fully armed and prepared, without saying to yourself, "Well, if I start getting a little nervous, I'll just make up an excuse and leave." It's difficult under such conditions to practice the QR. It's difficult to be tranquil when a good part of your mind is already focussed on the exit door.

It's far better—and really easier (although you may not believe it now)—to just burn all your bridges behind you!

Going Through a Setback

This phrase seems to be in common usage, but I often wonder if it isn't unnecessarily alarming. A setback implies setting yourself back—in other words, canceling out any gains made. And who wants to do that?

But think of it this way: Whatever progress is made is seldom, if ever, a complete success from start to finish. If you were to chart success on a graph, it would never be a straight up, up, up line. Rather, it would be like the stock market graphs you see in the newspapers—a series of wiggly lines going up and down, with plateaus in between. Yet, over the long haul (if you picked the right stock, that is), there would be a definite rise.

In nature, too, there are cyclical changes: the tides, day and night, the seasons, the weather. There is always ebb and flow, whether we're talking about electromagnetic waves or waves in the ocean. Everywhere you look you see this cyclical occurrence in nature. If this is true of nature, why shouldn't it be true of us? Aren't we part of nature?

So please don't be unduly alarmed if tomorrow you are not feeling as energetic as yesterday. Or if tomorrow it's a bit harder to do something that was easier last week. (This may be due to hormonal change—again, the cycle.) Consider this normal, and not deserving of the title "setback." Just accept this, and wait patiently for that upward swing again.

One more thing about setback. During and following a cold or the flu, you feel depressed. Depression is just part of the syndrome that goes with a cold or the flu—like aches and pains or fever. So it's nothing to worry about; it'll pass. The feeling of not wanting to do very much at this time (except just lying in bed passively) is nature's way of helping your body to rest and recover.

Any Roadblocks?

If, after following the program for a while, you still find it difficult to go out, our advice is to look for a roadblock. A roadblock is something that's obstructing your progress, something that gets in the way. Usually it's something minor, something that can easily be remedied.

What is it in your case? And how can you go about removing it? Think about it.

Ask yourself these questions:

Are my panic attacks helping me gain something I think I might otherwise not have (like people paying more attention to me)?

Do the panic attacks give me a legitimate excuse, a way out, to avoid doing something I really don't want to do?

Do I use the panic attacks as an excuse for not living up to my perfectionist standard? "Sure, if I didn't have the panic attacks, I could be (or do) such-and-such." Am I reluctant to give up this excuse because I *may* find out I'm really not so perfect or gifted after all?

If the answers to the above questions are yes, you can help yourself by thinking up *different ways* to meet those needs. After all, the underlying wishes of wanting a feeling of closeness with others, wanting to avoid overwhelming, problematic situations, wanting to be better, to improve—these are understandable human desires and nothing to be ashamed of. But one needn't use "sickness" as a means of meeting your needs. There are better and healthier ways to satisfy those desires.

Is It Ever Really Cured?

We have seen how panic attacks can start, how they can result from a combination of negative attitude, too much stress, poor health habits, a high sugar diet. We know there is a genetic predisposition. So you correct these lifestyle situations and the panic attacks go away.

But are you really cured? Or are the panic attacks merely arrested? Doesn't the genetic factor mean they could come back?

Yes, they could *if* you neglect your health again. *If* you go back to your old ways: too much stress, the wrong foods, pushing yourself beyond endurance. Yet even if this happens, even if the panic attacks do come back, you know what to do. It's no mystery anymore.

Remember this: The knowledge and strength you gained from this experience can never be lost. What you did before, you can do again!

What does it really mean to be cured? Does it mean never, ever being afraid? No. As long as there is life, there will be fear, doubt, insecurity. It's just the way life is.

So if you *are* sometimes fearful, sometimes insecure and worried—well, what of it? Welcome to the human race!

PART IV

TWENTY-FIVE PERSONAL STORIES—TOLD BY THE PEOPLE WHO LIVED THEM

Over the years, many of the people we have counseled at PASS-Group, Inc., have told us how helpful they have found hearing the stories of other people who have overcome their suffering from panic attacks. The twenty-five first-person accounts that follow were told to us by people we counseled at PASS-Group. To protect their identities, we have changed the names, but the stories are true. The first twenty stories appeared in the original edition of this book; the last five are new to this revised edition. The last is Shirley's own personal story. We hope that you find these accounts of triumph over suffering as inspiring as we have.

Alice's Story

I was born in Brooklyn. I grew up there and went to school there. Then, a few years after I got married, I moved to Vermont. That was about twenty years ago—and then the panic attacks began. I couldn't leave my home without suffering a severe panic attack. This prevented me from doing many things. I couldn't shop where I wanted; I couldn't even go to church. And I was extremely limited in the distance I could travel. At one point, I couldn't even go to the mailbox! My one wish was to be well enough to be able to come back to Brooklyn to visit my family.

Before the panic attacks began, I was the type of person who was always on the go. The attacks came in stages—first, I didn't want to go out alone; then, I couldn't go out at all, and finally, I became very uncomfortable even when I was alone in the house. My husband would tell people I was sick. It was very embarrassing to explain what was really wrong.

I was in private therapy for six years, without success. Then, finally, I couldn't see the point of sitting in a doctor's office week after week and just talking. I called the mental health clinic where I live, and they sent someone to my house to take me out a little. We would go out walking as far as I could go, and then we'd come back. I felt this was making progress, compared to the therapy.

But a few months later, while leafing through a *TV Guide*, I saw an ad for PASS and decided to give it a try. I started the program, and on August 16, 1983, just four months after I joined PASS, my wish to come to Brooklyn finally came true!

The trip coming down from Vermont was great. There were six of us in the car: my daughter, her husband (who was driving), their three children, and me. I found myself enjoying everything—the scenery, the ride. It was a long trip, so we stopped to eat several times along the thruway. I remember what my counselor said and didn't try to see the whole journey all at once, but broke it all down into small "baby" steps. Naturally, I was excited (who wouldn't be?), but I didn't think of it as nervousness—just a pleasant excitement and wonderful anticipation. After all, my dream of a lifetime was coming true!

Can you imagine how I felt when I finally saw the New York skyline? (The last time I saw it was in 1962!) After driving through Brooklyn, we went to Staten Island, where my brother now lives. Going over the Verrazano Bridge was especially thrilling for me because I used to live near the park that later became the base of the bridge. What a change in the old neighborhood! And what a reception I got at my brother's house! There was a huge banner on display that said, "Welcome Home Aunt Alice." But until they actually saw me stepping out of the car, my relatives couldn't believe I really made that trip!

That winter, back in Vermont, we were snowed in much of the time. But I had so many warm memories to remember about my trip to New York. I've since been on many other trips (including Brooklyn again), but this trip will always stand out as one of the highlights of my life.

I never think of my "phobia" anymore. I just think of good things when I go someplace. You have to try new things. If you don't, you miss out on a lot. And you never know you CAN, if you don't try.

What I learned is that I can do it. Life doesn't scare me anymore.

Bob's Story

I was eighteen years old, and I lived on a farm. I joined PASS because I had this terrified fear of leaving home. I wanted to learn to cope with problems and to find peace within myself.

The way my panic attacks started was this: I was with my cousin, and we went to a nearby town. We stopped over in a store, but on the way back—I don't know, out of nowhere (that's what really scared me!)—I got this enormous panic attack. But I couldn't go right back home. My cousin was driving and he had to make several stops. I felt real shaky and I was afraid of everything, because I had never experienced anything like this before. I couldn't understand what was happening to me. I thought I was going nuts—or dying or something!

That's when I started falling out of society; that was the beginning. Little by little, I began staying home. The more time went by, the more I'd stay home. I didn't really drop out of school at this point. I would *try* to go—but then I'd get panicky and have to run home. I didn't ask anybody; I'd just get in the car and leave. The principal knew I was having problems, and he was very good about it. I had started to see a psychologist at that time, and she helped me out by talking to the principal about me. But the more I would try to stay and fight—because I didn't know how to do it the *right* way— the worse it got.

That summer, to me, was a living hell. I didn't find out about PASS until December—and my panic attacks began in November, the year before. The second panic attack was when my buddy and I were drinking. After that episode, I never touched alcohol again. But things weren't so bad at the beginning—they just got progressively worse. Little by little, things started to go downhill. My car burned up, so I had no transportation other than my parents' car. My dad was very good about it—he let me use his car. But it just seemed that one thing after another went wrong. Things went down and down until I hit an all-time low. And then, little by little, I'd make a comeback. But I didn't have the information at that time that PASS later made available to me, and I didn't have the understanding to really get me back on my feet. I remember thinking that I didn't expect to live out the summer because I thought I was dying or going crazy, and I even thought of committing suicide!

And now that I *know* what I know, I can really look back and laugh at this! But you can't tell that to somebody who's just going through the first stages of this, because they're really scared. But I would say to them, once you get a better understanding of this, it just seems there's a whole new world opening up!

Do you know what I was eating before? A lot of sugar foods, a lot of candy bars, things like potato chips that were loaded with salt, french fries, things like that. I remember telling my counselor at the beginning of the program that I was on a very good diet! I *thought* I was, because I was also eating a lot of meat and potatoes. We've always raised our own beef on the farm, so I was brought up on a meat-and-potatoes diet. But now I'm eating five or six mini-meals and I watch what I eat. I really put together a very good diet now—and I exercise a lot. I'm in fantastic shape right now—I've never been in this good shape before!

Looking back, I see that I've made really great progress. For example, last week my mother and I got in the car and we went to this small town, about forty miles from here, to visit my mother's friend. And then, from there, we went to another town, about ten miles away. And then we went to the Capital City Mall. But that wasn't all: We went to *another* town, which is about twenty or thirty miles from here, and we shopped around. There are two malls there. Then, we went to a government surplus store, and had lunch at a very nice restaurant. On the way back, we stopped at a garage. There was a guy there who helped me get my car, and he was surprised to see me. And then we stopped at my buddy's trailer—and he also was surprised to see me.

And you know what my method is now? I just sit there and relax and let go—and I just think good thoughts and stuff. Like: How happy I am and how good life is—things like that. I look at the good.

What advice would I give to someone just starting this program? I would say, "Don't ever give up!" Because there were times when I thought seriously of committing suicide, things looked so bleak. I remember, at one point, I even planned on staying home the rest of my life . . . ! But I knew I could never do that. So don't you ever give up, either!

Brenda's Story

The panic attacks started about a month before I graduated from high school. I had just broken up with my boyfriend, so I was under great stress. I neglected my health, I didn't eat. Just knowing I was leaving high school, a secure place, and going out into the world—that, more or less combined with my personal problem—was what started the panic attacks.

I was in a very bad state. I was always having feelings of unreality. I was constantly living with this. I always used to think: Am I going to have a panic attack today? I hated to go too far from the house. I was worried I was going crazy. I was always thinking, always looking inward. Constantly. But the feelings of unreality worried me the most.

I think the basis for this worry is that people don't understand what's happening to them. So, in the back of their minds, they think something horrible is about to happen to them. Even when the doctor told me I was in excellent health, it didn't help at all. Nobody explained it to me before. I used to wonder: "What's the matter with me? Why am I like this?" So the worry continued. I remember once telling my doctor, "I don't feel like I'm really here." And he said, "Well, if you're not here, Brenda, where are you?" I didn't know at the time it's the body's way of working with stress. That's all it is. I also feel that when you're on a poor diet that has a lot to do with it. There's a biochemical disturbance that makes these feelings of unreality. And then, when you couple this with "inwardness," it only makes it worse, naturally. And then you really have a problem!

After I left high school, I got a job. I worked for this one company for two and a half years. Then my boyfriend and I (the one I had broken up with before) got together again. I had known him for a long time—we were childhood sweethearts—and he was pleading with me to go back with him. So I did—and we got married.

Six months later, I quit my job because I had to get up very early and hassle with buses, and so on—and it was just too much for me to handle. I had been taking buses in to work after I started getting panic attacks in the subway. The panic attacks were constantly on my mind. I wasn't able to go into a restaurant. I would get panic attacks just waiting for food to come. Then it went from restaurants to stores. I was getting panic attacks in stores, so I couldn't go into a store. The panic attacks soon stopped me from going to other places, too, like movies. It really restricted me because it spilled over into so many places.

I was in therapy before I joined this program. I had gone to a psychologist for over a year, and I wasn't getting anywhere. What he did for me was put me under hypnosis for about twenty minutes. That was very good. That was the only thing that was helpful—the relaxation. But here, with this program, I developed my own way of relaxing, my own technique. But, basically, at that point (when I was with the psychologist) I wasn't cured and I seemed to be getting nowhere. It was only after I joined this program that things really fell into place, with the change of diet, with the change in my attitude, with the relaxation, exercise, and so on. It was everything *combined*—*that* was the most important thing, that's what helped me.

At first, it was difficult to incorporate all these things into my lifestyle. But I was determined because I couldn't live like that anymore. I couldn't handle the constant fear on my shoulders. But getting back to the program—I knew I had to do things. I knew that the more I practiced, the more I'd get out of it. I hated to get in the car and go for an hour's drive. I started carrying the PASS book with me, carrying the tape with me (that was my little "security" then). This was after I'd been on the program—I'd say, about two months. I had a very poor diet before. I was eating a lot of things I wasn't supposed to, and I was eating a lot of sugar. No green vegetables, not enough protein—none of the things I was supposed to be eating.

It was a very gradual, not a sudden, improvement. I really think it was the combined approach that helped me. I can see now how everything works together—the seven steps. Because you apply each thing differently. Just having the knowledge of how your body/mind works—the nervous system and so on—gives you a better understanding of what's hap pening to you. Knowing what I'm supposed to eat—*that* makes a little less stress. Taking certain vitamins—*that* takes a chunk out of the stress. So, everything *combined* really diminishes anxiety.

My life is so different now from what it was! I look back in amazement! Being able to leave the house and not ever worrying about "what-if"; getting rid of that constant tension I had; just to leave the house and go to a store—it's wonderful! I think back—before, I used to make up so many excuses for not going out. And when I did go out, I could only go up to a certain point. And I also couldn't leave the house before 10:30 or 11 o'clock in the morning. Now, I can leave the house 8, 9—it doesn't matter. I don't have that time limit. And I go anywhere. I drive anywhere.

Before, I was so limited—I couldn't do many things. Now, I'm in and out of restaurants (only those with salad bars!). I take public transportation; I go shopping. In fact, I *love* to go shopping now. I usually go by myself or with my girlfriends. I drive my friends around from store to store, which gives me a *great* feeling. I always take food along when I'm driving. I might have a peach, yogurt, cantaloupe slices in a little container, cheese, whole wheat crackers, a container of soup. (Sometimes I think I could go on a two-week safari!) I just nibble along the way, as I go. By the way, I must say—not only didn't I gain weight using this method of frequent eating, but I lost six pounds!

Right now, my son is going to be in a play. He has rehearsals three times a week, so I take him and pick him up. I could let my husband do this, but, as I said, this gives me a great feeling, so I do it. I'm really enjoying this year's hustle and bustle, but I make the time to eat right, exercise, and—believe it or not—I relax in between.

I have a better way of coping with things now, a different way of looking at them. For example, last night I didn't get much sleep—only four hours. I had a slight headache (I know the reason) and my stomach was a little queasy. But even though it was queasy, I still had my egg on whole wheat toast and a cup of tea. Before the program, I would have had just toast and tea. But now I know what my body needs. I might have felt lightheaded before and not known what caused it. But now I realize it had a lot to do with my diet and my not eating whenever my stomach used to be a little upset. Because now I feel fine—no problem.

Here's another example: The other week, I went driving and I got lost. But I didn't panic, as I would have done before. I really didn't. In fact, I felt good and secure. I just told myself, "I can do it, I can find my way back." I didn't have anxiety about it. The thought now of panicking is very dim in my mind. I may *think* of it sometimes, but it's not at all like it used to be.

My husband was very supportive through all this. Sometimes we laughed together, sometimes we cried together. But this whole ordeal has brought us closer. Recently, I became a counselor for PASS. I enjoy helping people—and giving back to others what I was given.

Don's Story

The first time I had a full-fledged panic attack—I'll never forget it—was one night after I left work. I was walking down the street and it felt like somebody had hit me over the head, it was that sudden. My heart started pounding, my legs turned to jelly, I couldn't breathe—the whole bit. This got me into an anxiety state for weeks. Finally, after a couple of weeks of this constant anxiety, I confided in a friend of mine, who happens to be a therapist. And she referred me to a psychiatrist. So I went into therapy and that lasted two years.

Although I got a lot out of the therapy itself—for instance, I learned a lot about myself; it forced me to look at and resolve a lot of the conflicts in my life—it didn't help me as far as the panic attacks were concerned. It didn't give me the practical knowledge I needed in order to deal with the panic attacks. My most feared experience was driving through the tunnel and getting stuck in traffic there. One day this happened—and I thought I was going to stop breathing. It was nighttime, it was dark, and I felt just like getting out and running. It was total *panic!*

So it wasn't until I got involved with PASS that I really felt it was going to get better. The information that my counselor gave me was basic, concrete, common sense information. I didn't have to take apart my mother, my father, and this and that, to try to find out how to resolve something. I remember being so surprised when my counselor cut me short the first time I started talking about my mother, my childhood. Because I thought that was what you were supposed to say. I was in therapy at the time, and that, basically, was the vehicle they used.

I stopped smoking over a year ago. That was one of the things I wanted to do—and I finally did it. I must say, I feel *so* much better! I'll never go back to smoking. I gained weight—I was much too thin before—and I exercise, I work out. I feel really good—and I look a lot better, too.

I learned two important things from my experience with the panic attacks: (1) Perseverance. You have to stick with it. And (2) Patience. Coming from that experience, these are two things that stayed with me, that have become part of my coping skills.

I recently went into business, but the business failed. This set me back a bit, financially. But I'm young—I'm in my thirties. And I learned a lot from this experience. I realized some of the mistakes I made. So I'm going to try again soon. Nowadays, I don't give up that easily. I know that, in time, I'll make it.

My message to someone suffering from panic attacks is this: You really can get beyond it and over it. I think the key word is "acceptance." The moment I accepted the way it was, it changed everything for me for the better. That's another paradox, isn't it? But I think it's because you're taking the pressure off yourself. As soon as you say it's OK to be this way, you're freeing yourself. Instead of saying, "I wish I were different" or "I wish I felt differently," you say, "This is the way I'm feeling and I'm going to accept that fact." By doing that, you take a tremendous weight off your shoulders. Because you don't have to force yourself to change; the change happens naturally.

It takes time. My improvement was gradual. That's how I learned to be patient and to stick with it. You can't give up on yourself.

Elaine's Story

My story begins five years ago, in a car. I had been having a rushed day of shopping with my sister and when I turned to go home, the road looked strange. I wasn't sure where we actually were. After I made several turns (I was driving), a panic attack just hit me out of the blue! After I pulled off the road, we got a police car to stop and help, and I was taken to the emergency room of a nearby hospital.

Up until then, hyperventilation wasn't even a word in my vocabulary—and I know how casually people use this term. But I experienced it to the point of total stiffness throughout my body. After a similar occurrence in a shopping mall and a return to the hospital emergency room, the doctor sent me for extensive testing for possible ear problems.

When these tests came back negative, I was told to see a psychologist. I worked with him for a couple of months. It did help some, but not enough to bring me back to the so-called "normalness" of before.

If you've never experienced this personally, it's very hard for anyone to actually relate to those feelings that came over me. Feelings of complete panic would set in with no warnings at all—or so it seemed. To venture out alone was impossible. I began to plan all my trips away from the house with my husband, because it was "safe" when I was with him. A trip to the grocery store was a grueling adventure. I would go down each aisle and hope there was no one there I knew so that I wouldn't have to stop and talk. The checkout line loomed ahead of me a mile long, and it felt like my legs didn't want to hold me up.

At church, just trying to sit in a pew and watch the usher rope off the back pews was unbearable. At one service, we had to get up and leave. The noise level of crowds tripled to my ears. Sometimes, I could hardly stand the sounds of people altogether.

But my main problem was driving a car alone. It seemed it took more patience than I could muster to stay at an inter-section and wait out the panic scene in my head. I can still re-member vividly sitting at the light stop, waiting for left turns and trying to make sense of everything around me (those lights seemed *days* long!). The muscles of my legs and body were so tensed up all the time that I wonder now how on earth I could even have walked by myself! And the fact that I had no idea what was really going on was frightening. I was afraid to talk to anyone about these feelings. Who could pos-sibly understand what was going on in my head?

When my husband saw something in the paper about PASS, he showed it to me and I sent away for information. And that eventually led me on the road to recovery. Let me tell you that without the help and understanding of my counselor, Jaye, I don't know what condition I'd be in today! On Saturdays, we had our telephone sessions, and I always looked forward to that. I was all ears and very eager to listen to every word she said. I did exactly as she told me, with full confidence. I thought if she got well, then I would, also. I learned exactly what was happening to me and I started to put the whole picture together.

The main changes in my life have been to learn to relax, to change my way of acting *completely*, and just to learn to slow down and live. The trick in learning to relax to the fullest is to *practice.* I do the relaxation tape almost daily, so now my body is tuned to relax completely at a given signal. I abstain from all forms of sugar (other than what's in fruit, etc.). This helped "stabilize" my blood sugar and enabled me to have a more steady feeling. I eat plain old, good food—fruits, vegetables, fish, chicken, yogurt, and some red meat occasionally. Whole grain breads and crackers are now staples in my diet. Since I found caffeine to be intolerable to my system, I eliminated it. After many months on this diet, my weight dropped and I feel so much stronger and better. The weight loss is an added benefit.

Frank's Story

I'm a free-lance writer and I also write music—so my life is riddled with stress and tension, as far as that's concerned. You've heard of a Type A personality? Well, I'm a Triple-A personality!

My life, before I started this program, was intolerable. I was in persistent and lengthy states of tension and anxiety. It was a living hell. As far as I'm concerned, I was one step away from needing to be locked up! I was living in fear constantly; I really considered I was having a nervous breakdown! I couldn't sleep nights. It was difficult for me to commit myself to anything—social or in business—because of my panic attacks. I used to be frightened of every new symptom—especially in my chest and head. These severe symptoms dominated me and stifled my goals in life. I was overly conscious of doing, eating, or thinking about anything that might add stress or cause one of these attacks that I was constantly on my guard against. I desperately sought ways to control these symptoms and I needed constant reassurance that I was not in any physical or medical danger. Yet I wanted very much to be able to resume living, enjoying life and pursuing my goals without being constantly on guard. One day, my girlfriend showed me an article in *Family Circle* magazine that mentioned PASS, and that's how I joined the program.

I live in New York, and my recent trip to California was probably the highlight, the culmination of my endeavors. You might think it was pretty daring on my part, but my "secret" was to stop viewing it as something daring! The thing is to break the habit of viewing something as being an obstacle or being something huge. For example, one day I had to take a bus to New Jersey and that was sort of the first big barrier since I'd gotten into the bad habit of sitting around at home all the time, thinking that I was "ill" and couldn't go anywhere. Anyhow, I had to go to New Jersey and I really just relaxed and had a very smooth time with that trip—it involved a long subway ride followed by a long bus ride. I brought my music along, to listen to. And once I was on the bridge going to New Jersey, I thought it was great. I realized if I could do this successfully, I knew I was capable of going to California. And from that point on, whenever I thought of going to California, the phrase that I used for myself was: "I'm in the same physical condition, the same physical health, whether I'm in New York or in Montana or on Mars!" And if I remembered that and accepted that and believed it, then there was no reason to even think that just by going a distance away, anything "physical" was going to happen. Of course, the logical aspect came to me pretty quickly, but the practice of applying it—that took a little while.

Of course, I had a lot of "anticipatory anxiety" about the trip. But once I was on the plane, it was fine. I used the whole arsenal of "tools" I acquired through the program and Dr. Weekes's books; I used them whenever I grew anxious or tense. I sat next to the window and watched the takeoff. Wow! And I remember, on the way back from California, we were flying just as the sun was rising above the clouds. It was just exhilarating and so beautiful to sit there and look out of the window and watch the clouds and the sky light up and turn a beautiful shade of blue. It was just wonderful!

There was one point when the plane had to drop a little bit to get out of some clouds, and my stomach was up in my throat for a few seconds. But the first thing I did, under the circumstances, was the QR. I took a couple of deep abdominal breaths and just told myself to do all the right things in terms of physical relaxation. And I was just fine within a matter of a few seconds. So everything was very successful, in terms of dealing with the anxiety.

Another valuable thing about taking that trip to California is that I can now recall some of the more wonderful aspects of travel. Anyone with the problem of agoraphobia should look forward to tackling a little expedition, because you can use that as your visualization exercise. Like the time I went to the beach or the time I was up in a plane, looking at the clouds. Those mental "photographs"—while I enjoyed those situations, I also use them now in conjunction with my relaxation tape. When you recall or recapture something that was enjoyable to you, it not only benefits you in terms of your immediate bodily reactions, but it also provides that stimulus to go out and do again—and do more.

I'm still under a lot of stress—I'm always having to meet deadlines, etc.—but it doesn't get to the point of panic anymore. I just view those certain periods as times when I just have to be patient with myself. Now that I have this different approach to my work, I take periodic exercise breaks—*before* the tension builds up. I might do some stretching or some light calisthenics or dance very gently to radio music for a while (it depends on what I feel comfortable with) on any given day. Or I might do more strenuous things—like two days ago, I had all this energy, so I was out playing basketball. I kept going at it for a while, but I felt great. I'm in very good condition again, now that I've been exercising regularly. While I was in California, I played tennis with my friends, and I was as effective as ever on the tennis court. I'm really trim now, although I was never heavy. I noticed I'm in considerably better shape than the last time I was in California.

When I joined the PASS program, I was already on medication, but I was still getting panic attacks *all the time!* Now, since I started the PASS program, I decreased my dosage. In fact, during my trip to California, I cut it down even more. And I've not had anything even *resembling* panic in quite some time. I really feel I'm dealing very effectively with the whole situation. Just by diet, exercise, attitude change, and so on, and practicing to deal with any symptoms as soon as they happen. My girlfriend noticed the changes in me a lot more than anyone else because she was living with me when my condition had reached its "peak." One day, while I was in California, she was telling my other two friends—and she was beaming when she said it—"Oh, it's so great to see the change in him. He's actually able to sit in a restaurant and have a meal!" And: "He's able to just turn off the TV and come to sleep at night." Before, I had a very big problem with sleeping. The insomnia was simply unbearable.

So you see I'm a strong advocate of this entire program—because I've seen for myself what it can do!

Gloria's Story

I began having panic attacks in 1969, after I went through an extremely emotionally stressful period. The doctor put me on Valium at the time and I took the medication for five years. Then I went to another doctor, who took me off the Valium and prescribed a different kind of medication, to be taken only as needed. I never went out much then, because whenever I'd go to a crowded public place, my chest would start pounding and I'd start trembling.

I joined PASS in November of 1984 because my son was going to be married in March and I was literally walking around in a nightmare: I worried—How was I ever going to go to the wedding? What would I do when I panicked? I had been desperately looking for a program that would help me get through that day in one piece! I didn't want to be knocked out by pills. Of course, my ultimate goal was to be able to go anywhere by myself, with confidence and in control of myself, without panicking or becoming frightened.

Soon after I started the PASS program, I began to make the necessary changes in my lifestyle. I had been on a liquid diet, eating only one little meal a day, in order to lose ten pounds before the wedding. I stopped this diet and went on the one recommended by PASS. At the end of November, I started my program of regular exercise. I was very careful about my diet now and also about the relaxation exercises. There were a lot of people in my exercise class, and I was pleasantly surprised that I didn't feel any of the panic I used to feel in crowds.

By December, I was already feeling much better. Even my husband noticed the difference and remarked how much calmer I had become. By Christmas, I was beginning to feel a lot more optimistic about the turnaround in my life. I had some stress—some family problems at that time—but I found I really changed my outlook on things. My attitude was different now. I let things ride and I wasn't as "all strung out" as I used to be. So the stress didn't affect me that much and I was able to cope. I also became more involved socially with the women's group of my husband's lodge.

In January, we began getting ready for the wedding in March. I talked to my counselor about being nervous at the wedding, but she somehow reassured me that all would be well. I did my relaxation session faithfully every day. We were getting a lot of phone calls now, so I used to take the phone off the hook for that half hour. In mid-January, I suddenly felt ill. I thought it might be nerves, but when I saw the doctor, he told me it was an intestinal virus. I decided not to pay attention to it, and it just cleared up by itself. I used the "worry-hour" strategy. Whenever I wanted to worry about the wedding or something else, I'd postpone the worry for a few hours and worry about it all at once. It worked for me—and I found I could relax a lot better during the day.

I had another goal before the wedding: to be able to go shopping in Bloomingdale's. So one day, I went there with my future daughter-in-law. Once in the store, I was really surprised that I didn't feel closed in, the way I used to feel. I only had a little mild fluttering in my stomach, but after a few moments it went away. I knew how to handle it.

The bridal shower was held at my house. A few days before, I called my counselor at PASS because I was getting anxious. She reassured me and told me it was perfectly normal. She advised me to do most of the cooking and baking the day before—even to clean the house before—so the day of the party all would be in order and I wouldn't have anything hanging over my head. Well, it just went beautifully. Everything was lovely. This success gave me more courage to face the wedding. And, as it turned out, I also didn't have to worry about the wedding: Everything turned out wonderful.

The weather was lovely, the bride was lovely. I wore a beige gown that really looked great on me. I also had my makeup put on by a professional—I felt like a movie star! I was so excited, but it was a happy excitement. About 300 people attended the wedding. The main event for me was when we all walked into the ballroom and they introduced us. I had a wonderful time. The evening went by so fast, I couldn't believe it. It was 2 A.M. when it was all over.

I feel this program helped me a lot. It made me realize so many things. I'm more aware now. I know what can bring on a panic attack and I see that doing the right things helps me avoid the panic attack. I go to a lot of places by myself now. There's a big shopping mall near me and I now go there all the time. (It's really within walking distance, so I often walk there.) Before, when I had to go there, I'd hurry up with everything just to get it over with. But now I go there leisurely. I take my time, look around, and I really enjoy it.

Now, whenever I go somewhere, I tend not to think "what if this, what if that." I just go where I have to go.

Helene's Story

One New Year's Day, I had a panic attack, but I didn't know what it was. I thought I was just overtired because I had been up late New Year's Eve. So it didn't upset me. (Later, I found out my intuition was right!) I didn't have another panic attack until two months later, when I went to a car show with my husband. We were walking around, and I started having these "funny feelings." I thought I was going to faint, that's how I felt. And I thought it was because I was smelling the car exhaust fumes (again, my intuition was probably correct). Anyhow, we went home; I rested a while, and I was fine. Then, in May of that year, I was in an accident where I got hit on the head. Two days later, I was with the kids in school—I'm a teacher—and they were watching a play. During the play, I had those "funny feelings" again; I thought I was going to faint. I felt really shaky, very nervous and dizzy. My first reaction was to get out of there, to get out of that room. I felt I needed fresh air. Another teacher saw me and said to me, "You better go to the doctor now and find out what's wrong with you." She knew I had the accident with my head, and she told me it might be very serious.

So I left my class with a substitute, and I went to the doctor. While driving to his office, I had the worst panic attack ever. I almost couldn't drive the car. I was so afraid I might pass out while driving and be in another accident again. And I was also nervous about going to the doctor. I wondered what he might find. So these fears were just building up inside of me, making everything worse.

As it turned out, the x-rays were normal and the doctor found I was all right physically. A few months later, though, I had another panic attack that came out of the blue. I started having a couple of panic attacks a week, and sometimes I'd even have two or three during the day. I realized something wasn't right. So I went to the doctor again. He checked me out thoroughly and prescribed Xanax, a very mild prescription. He tried to figure out something in my life that was causing stress and starting these attacks, but we couldn't figure out anything. He thought maybe it was something I was not consciously aware of yet.

At first, I wasn't taking the pills right, because I didn't think I needed to be taking pills; you always hear these terrible stories about people becoming addicted to them. Well, the panic attacks kept recurring, so finally I did begin to take the pills regularly. But even though I was now taking the pills the way I was supposed to, the panic attacks still crept up on me.

My mother, who knew what was going on all this time, saw an article in the paper, written by a doctor, about PASS. I kept the paper, but I still didn't call. I waited. Then, school was about to start again, but there was no way I could teach, the way I felt. The panic attacks kept happening more and more, and the pills were hardly working. So at that point, I called PASS and I started the program.

What I liked about this program from the start was its common-sense approach, and its one-to-one counseling. And there were steps you could take right away. Like the eating—that helped a lot. Right away, I started eating every three hours and watched what I ate. And I really noticed the difference. I started the exercise, to a certain extent, before I began the PASS program. But when I realized how important it was, I just kept it up. And the relaxation tape helped a lot. I really didn't know how tense I was until I started listening to the tape and realized afterwards how much tension I had accumulated during the day.

You know, one of my biggest problems—believe it or not—was when I had to have my hair cut. I've been going to this girl for two years, but I had a big panic attack there once, so every time I went back, it reminded me. So it wasn't easy going back. My counselor suggested that right after I listened to the relaxation tape, I should visualize being at the beauty parlor and go through each little step in a relaxed way, in my imagination. So I did that for the four days before my appointment. It happened to be at the beginning of the PASS program, when I was really scared about getting my hair cut. Well, just before I went there, I had butterflies in my stomach. But that was the extent of it. That was it. I didn't have any "funny feelings" or anything like that. When I left the beauty parlor, I called up my counselor and yelled, "I did it! I can't believe I did it!" I was so excited and thrilled. And then, another time after that, I was in the beauty parlor to get a perm, and I was there for something like three hours. And it worked out fine, too. I really believe that visualization is a very helpful method—because it's like a dress rehearsal.

Looking back on this whole experience with panic attacks, I can see now that my biggest problem was that I was exaggerating the weird feelings I was having—whereas I should have just ignored them and realized that I was going to be all right. If I had known that from the beginning—instead of always worrying that something was seriously wrong with me—I would have relaxed, and it wouldn't have developed into such a big problem.

Jason's Story

My first memories of panic attacks go back to 1975; I had two or three within a couple of weeks, on the subway. A little while after that, I was taking a shower, and after the shower, I passed out. Fortunately, I was able to jump out of the shower when I started feeling dizzy and lightheaded. But by the time I was starting to dry myself off, I was "out." And from that point on, for some reason, every physical sensation that I had was very heightened. And I started noticing that I was getting very tense. Pretty soon after that, I had another panic attack. And at that point, I really got worried. I had been dieting very heavily and hadn't been eating—but I still didn't understand what was happening. I was actually hoping that this was something physical that I could take care of.

I went to my family doctor and he gave me a full physical checkup. He told me I was perfectly normal and that this was just "nerves." So that really started the whole process of thinking it's "mental." I said to myself: OK, what's wrong with me? Why did I have a nervous reaction? I started to analyze everything. I thought: My life seemed normal. So it must be that I'm going crazy or cracking up inside. There must be this dark, deep thing inside that's causing me to have these terrible feelings, I thought. But I didn't share that with anyone and things got worse.

Well, I did a pretty good job of hiding it. I didn't like to admit that things were going wrong, so I let it sit with me as long as I possibly could. And that started to include whole evenings when I would just be feeling very tense; everything seemed a little weird and out of focus. Once, I went to a sporting event in mid-Manhattan, and the minute I got into the arena, I felt very disoriented. For that whole evening, I didn't know what was going on. I just knew I was very nervous and thought that something bad might happen any minute. I was with a friend, so of course I didn't say anything. I sort of sat there, gritting my teeth and counting the minutes till I could leave.

I had been seeing a therapist when this incident happened, but I didn't even tell him about some of the stuff that had been happening. I hid it from him, too, because I guess I was embarrassed. I had a lot of trouble admitting weakness. Because at that time I had interpreted all this as a kind of "weakness" on my part. And at the beginning stages I really didn't believe it was a physical thing. So I didn't share it with anyone and things got worse.

Well, I wound up jumping from doctor to doctor. For example, I went to a neurologist and had an EEG. Then I went to an ophthalmologist because the symptoms seemed to be vision-related. I had disorientation and blurred vision at times. But everything checked out OK. My parents encouraged me to go to doctors because they were convinced I'd find a cure.

Finally, my girlfriend heard about PASS on the radio and she told me to call the number. I was very hesitant. But I was kind of at my wit's end because I had exhausted the channels of dealing with it on my own.

At the time I called PASS, I wouldn't even go to a movie; I would hesitate to even drive. After a couple of telephone sessions, they gave me so much information that I never even heard of before: that what I had was common; that I wasn't "going crazy"; that there was an actual basis for this, and so on. It was the first time that anything made sense to me, really. There was a kind of cohesiveness to the whole thing. It was also great to have a male counselor and to hear that he had it, too, at one time. Because most of the information I was getting was that it was only a female-oriented kind of problem. Certainly, in light of my difficulty in admitting weakness, having a male counselor gave me a bit of momentum and impetus to improve.

Basically, my life has changed very much since I took the program. I don't get really worried now about doing anything. And there's nothing that I stop myself from doing if I want to do it. I also understand that I'm not going to be totally "worry-free" for the rest of my life. But I don't feel "alone." I know what this is all about and I feel that I'm now in charge of my life. I've gone back to school to get my B.S. This was something I really wanted to do, but I lacked the confidence before. I had doubts about my ability; I didn't know I could do it. But then, once this business with the panic attacks cleared up, I decided to go for it. I'm getting very good grades and I'll be getting my M.S.W. next year.

When I graduate, I'd love to hook myself up with a clinic or mental health facility that deals with phobic individuals. I want to help people—especially those who have this problem. I feel "all together" now. I have a much broader perspective on things and I'm much more confident because I've already overcome so many hurdles myself.

Marla's Story

My problem with panic attacks started when I stayed home for a couple of years with my second child when he was a baby. That's when I had a lot of time to sit and think. I felt very isolated. I didn't have many friends then. I know that introspection is a common problem with people who have panic attacks, and that they're usually creative people. So they need other interests. I think I did have many other interests on and off before, but during those few years when I was home, I didn't. And so the jogging I started doing for exercise helped me get started again. It gave me the incentive I needed to get out of the house again and start doing things. Then, later, I got a part-time job, and that helped rebuild my confidence, too.

I had been bothered by panic attacks, actually, since I was fifteen (I'm thirty now). I was determined to find out what the heck it was. I read whatever I could find on it, but I never quite pinpointed it. I used to try to find out in my own little way if anybody else experienced this. But when I'd ask, they'd say, "Oh, I know what you mean. Everybody gets nervous once in a while." But I knew they didn't quite know what I meant. Yet, the funny part of it is that now that I *know* what it is, a few people have mentioned it to *me*.

I guess I was more fortunate than most, because the panic attacks never kept me home. With me, I never associated the panic attacks with the outdoors. Instead, the panic attacks would occur indoors—especially when I was home during those few years with my son. I started being afraid of doing things I normally used to do—like going shopping alone. Whenever I'd be in the store, I'd get that uncomfortable, panicky feeling and I'd want to leave right away.

When I first read the newspaper article about a girl who suffered from panic attacks, I couldn't believe how it described me to a T. Then, at the end of the article, it listed places where you could get help, and that's how I found PASS. What I liked about this program was that there was no medication involved. And it was done over the phone—it wasn't like you had to travel every week.

For me, the program was fairly easy to follow because I'm very disciplined about my eating habits. But I must admit that the one thing I found difficult was staying away from coffee, because I enjoy drinking coffee; I love the taste of it. So now, if I do have a little coffee now and then and find myself a little bit nervous from it or "hyper," I know why it's happening, so it doesn't bother me.

One of the best parts of the program for me was just finding out about this group and having someone explain to me exactly what I was feeling. *Why* the panic attacks were happening and what I could do about it. What's important is that you're able to slow your body down. You're more in control. Like when you feel a panic attack coming on, knowing that you can take a deep breath and do some other relaxation technique and that, just physically alone, it's going to slow you down. And knowing that when you're getting the attack, that that's the worst that can happen—that it's not going to get any worse than that. All these things are important. I started the program over a year ago, and I haven't had any panic attacks for a long time now (knock wood!). Naturally, I feel a little bit more nervous at times, but this just tells me I have to slow down a bit—and I do. But just knowing that if I get a panic attack, I can handle it seems to stop them from coming.

Nancy's Story

Before I was on this program, I used to get three or four severe panic attacks a week. Then, after I was on the program a while, the panic attacks would only get so bad; they weren't at all like they used to be, in intensity. And most of the time, I knew I'd brought it on myself. But it's much easier to deal with when you know *you're* doing it than if it's something "out there." So the panic attacks certainly weren't as severe as before. And then I would start getting them right before my period, sort of in clusters. I'd also be a little blue just before my period, a little dizzy. I'd cry easily or I'd fly off the handle at the least little thing.

When I went to my gynecologist, I showed him this PASS course. I showed him the diet and everything, and told him what I was doing. He said, "Keep on with that diet." He explained that it takes a longer time when you're doing something nutritionally. It's not like when you take a pill and it's designed to clear everything up right away. But when you're doing things nutritionally, he said, it may take a matter of months. So I knew it was a process.

How is it now? This month, I didn't even know my period was coming—until I looked at the calendar! I'm sure it's due to the diet and the exercise. Because I remember that when I was in high school and we had exercise in gym, I never had cramps or any of those other symptoms. But after the children were born, I became more sedentary. I wasn't getting the exercise I used to get. And then you're so busy with the children, you pop anything in your mouth for lunch—or you even skip lunch altogether. I remember having ice cream for lunch, just to get a quick lift. Now, of course, I watch what I eat and I exercise regularly, so that's what I think made the difference.

After being on the program a while, I began to notice differences about me. And my husband noticed them, too. I used to dread getting up in the morning. When the alarm would go off, I'd feel sick. I used to say, "Oh, no . . . ! Another day . . . ! I'm going to die today, for sure . . . !" It's nothing like that now. When I get up now, I feel *great!* I don't feel like I'm schlepping around the house. I get up, I take my shower, make my breakfast, get the kids ready—and we go out. I'm living a *normal* life!

What can I do now that I wasn't able to do before? I couldn't go out by myself before. And if I did go out with somebody—let's say, we were in a department store—if they moved away from me, even just to check something out at the next counter, I would panic immediately. Now, last week, for example, I went to Macy's alone. I bought some crystal and I also bought myself a hat for a wedding I'm going to on Saturday (I'm a "hat freak"; I love hats). I just went and did it—no problem! I could *never* do that before.

I also couldn't be left alone. When I was alone in the house—and, technically, I really wasn't alone; I had my two small children, my cats and my dog!—I would break out into a sweat. I'd start "what-iffing." I'd think, "Now, what if I have an attack and I pass out here on the floor . . . ?" Or: "What if this is the Big One?" Now, it's almost a blessing to be all alone in the house when the kids aren't here.

Pete's Story

I'm a manager and, before I joined the PASS program, I'd work anywhere from seventy to eighty hours a week—sometimes even up to one hundred hours a week! In addition to my long hours, there was an awful lot of pressure on the job. Most of the time, I'd have to work under time deadlines. The hardest thing was working without adequately trained people—and good people were hard to get. I live in an area where the unemployment rate is very, very low—less than three percent. In fact, we've had to bus people in from other areas to come and work in Rhode Island. So, without proper help, my job was that much more difficult.

My diet was pretty awful, too—mostly junk food. I would often skip breakfast altogether. And sometimes I didn't have a chance to eat at all until 6 o'clock at night. So I went without eating a meal, from dinner the night before. Many times, I'd just have snacks—potato chips, soda, things like that. If I had lunch, it usually consisted of sandwiches or a roll or white bread, with chicken or roast beef, and I'd wash it down with ginger ale or Hi-C.

But I've completely changed all that now. I eat a good breakfast. I eat all my meals—and I have decent meals. I stopped having junk food. I got myself on a well-balanced diet.

I've also cut down on my workload a lot. I requested and finally got another assistant. And this time they gave me qualified people. Before, I had basically new people who weren't as familiar with the job. Right now, I'm working no more than fifty hours a week. My workload is way down—almost cut in half, compared with what it was before.

When I joined PASS, I was very nervous—and not only at work. I couldn't go to a restaurant. I wasn't able to go shopping. I just avoided most situations. But my goal was to live a normal life; to be able to go out to a restaurant now and then and attend meetings and go shopping.

And now I can do all that. I can just about go anywhere and do anything. I don't get panic attacks or anything like that anymore. I can go to restaurants. In fact, just yesterday, we went to a restaurant and it was very nice. I enjoyed myself (and, of course, I ordered the right foods). In previous times, whenever I had to handle something personal, some crisis that was very stressful, I'd find it very difficult to deal with. Last week, there was a death in the family; my wife's father passed away. My wife was the oldest daughter, so there were many things we had to do. I did everything I had to, and my wife was surprised that I was able to handle the crisis and all that stress so well, without any adverse effects whatsoever. I see now that when your diet is better and when you're in better physical shape, you're able to handle much more stress.

If you're new to the program, my one word of advice is to keep an open mind. Don't go into the program thinking this isn't going to work. Or thinking: How can changing my diet and things like that help me or have such a calming effect or cure me—because my panic attacks are so intense. This program definitely *can* help. It's changed the course of my life considerably. I can pretty much do anything I want to now, without the fear of having a panic attack hanging over my head.

Phyllis's Story

I've had panic attacks since childhood, since I was about sixteen. They seemed to come out of nowhere. I remember the first time it happened: My heart suddenly started beating very fast and I felt like I couldn't breathe. The next time it happened, I was in school, and it was so bad, I had to go home. And then, when it happened after that, my parents took me to a hospital. The doctors examined me thoroughly and said it was "just nerves." I used to have air-hunger all the time—I'd gasp for air and I'd start to hyperventilate. And it used to bother me. I'd keep asking myself, "Why do I have to breathe like this?"

After I finished high school, I went to college. But, for a number of reasons—not only because of the panic attacks—I dropped out of school and got a job. I worked at a few jobs. Then I got a job as a waitress right across the street from where I live. I took the job because I figured, in case I get a panic attack, I can just run right home. Anyhow, I worked there for four years. But the panic attacks were getting progressively worse. They were always bad, but it was during the past three years that I could say the fear was just taking control of my life.

That's when I started seeing a psychologist. I wasn't in treatment long—only a couple of months. But there was no improvement. In fact, I was getting worse because I was constantly thinking about the panic attacks. The psychologist used to have me write down all my thoughts and feelings in a little book that I used to carry around with me everywhere I went. But that only made me focus even more on my problem. So that didn't work at all.

While I was still seeing my psychologist, I happened to read an article in the Sunday *News* about fear—and at the end of the article, they listed places where you could get help. That's where I first learned about the PASS program.

Changing my attitude has helped me the most. The turning point came for me when I was talking one night to Cindy, my counselor. She said I really had to start getting myself occupied and to stop worrying about how the other people on the program were coming along. Because at that point I knew all of my teammates were doing a lot better. And it bothered me that out of the four of us, I was the one who was in pretty bad shape. That conversation with my counselor was the turning point for me, because it was then that I decided that I wasn't going to worry about anybody else and how they were progressing. Not that I didn't care; but I wasn't going to worry anymore that they were coming along faster than I was. I decided to stop comparing myself to them. And I didn't care if it took me a year, two years—I would recover in my own time.

And that was when I started going to church more often. One night, I was outside the church, talking to a girl I had just met. I was asking her all kinds of questions about the church, its beliefs, etc. Then this man joined us, and I told him about the panic attacks. And what this man said made such an impression on me! He said, "God didn't create you with a spirit of fear." He showed me the Bible, where Jesus says: "Peace I leave with you. Let not your heart be troubled, neither let it be afraid." I started to cry because, at that point, I really started to believe that what he was saying was true. I thought that no matter how long it would take for me to get better, I knew that this was the way I would do it. I would put my life in God's hands and allow Him to lead me.

Now, when I do all those things I used to be afraid of doing,

I have faith that God is with me. And *I am able to do those things.* I am working now. I am going out. I'm driving. I'm just doing everything. And I don't get panic attacks anymore. Once in a while, I might feel those little feelings come up, but I put my mind back on God—and the fear just goes away!

If I could give just one bit of advice to someone suffering from panic attacks, I would say this: You have to change your attitude. You have to believe in something. In my case, it's God.

Regina's Story

When I first joined the PASS program, I was very incapacitated by agoraphobia. I had suffered with this for many, many years. I was sixty-two when I joined the program. Although I was able to ride in a car, I could not stay in a store for more than fifteen minutes. Beyond that time, it was impossible. I had been in therapy with a psychiatrist, but there was no improvement.

Then, one day I saw an ad for PASS in *TV Guide.* I joined the program—and I never believed I'd get this far, but I did. I remember the first time I did something daring—and this was after I had been on the program for three months. (It was my biggest adventure in eighteen years!)

I have my hair done every week. My hairdresser, a lovely young woman, used to come to my house. One day, she told me she was getting married—and I received an invitation in the mail. The wedding was in September; I had started the program in June. But I was making such good progress with the program that I decided to go. I even went to a store (one of my "assignments") to buy a wedding present. When my daughter saw it, she offered to take it to the wedding, but I said, "Oh, no, you won't—I'm taking it myself." At first, she thought she heard wrong. She asked me, "Do you think you can?" I said, "I *know* I can!"

On the day of the wedding, as I was getting dressed, I was very nervous (the bride wasn't the only one!). But my faith in the program and the knowledge that I could do it helped me through. I sat—not in the back of the church, but right in the middle! The altar was beautifully decorated with flowers; it was a lovely ceremony.

The next step was the reception. I had come this far, and I knew I could stay. I sat down with a roomful of people (there were about one hundred guests) and enjoyed a delicious turkey dinner (of course, I didn't touch the dessert!). After they cut the cake, the dancing began—and I danced a few times (my husband isn't much for dancing). The bride was so happy to see me at her wedding. She asked jokingly, "Does this mean I'm fired?" And I told her proudly that from now on, she could expect me to be coming to *her* at the beauty parlor every week! I was very happy when I got home because I knew I had done something far beyond my dreams.

What else do I do now that I wasn't able to do before? Well, I'm back at church. I used to be a regular church member years ago, but when I had agoraphobia, then of course I couldn't go. One day I just decided I was able to go and I wanted to go, so I went, and I kept on going! I attend service regularly now, and I like it very much. It brings me great satisfaction.

This summer, I've been going some weekends to visit my daughter. She has a camper in a trailer park and it's a two-hour drive from my house. I can go to the stores now—and to big shopping malls. I went to a mall last week with 88 stores in it and it didn't bother me at all. I was there over two hours.

I've been to Canada recently to visit my sister. We went shopping there all day, and it didn't bother me. Traveling doesn't bother me at all now. I can travel anywhere and I can go to restaurants, which I certainly wasn't able to do before. I haven't had a panic attack in a long time, not in ages and ages! And I never thought I'd be doing the things I'm doing now!

Rita's Story

My panic attacks started when I was in high school. I was seventeen at the time, and that was a long time ago. I was bothered for a little while, but then the panic attacks left me, and they didn't occur again until years later.

It was never that I couldn't go out of the house or anything like that; it wasn't that severe. I didn't know what it was *at all*. I was just very nervous and panicky. I would just get nervous about things, but nothing happened to me, so I sort of "got out of it."

Then, as I said, years later, a couple of things happened that triggered these feelings again that I had almost forgotten about. It was just that different things were going on at once: I had been dating somebody for a pretty long time, and we broke up. Then, my mother got sick—things like that. But this time—the second time I had it—I was more conscious of what was happening. I knew I wasn't "different." I realized these feelings were being triggered by a lot of the stuff that was going on in my life.

It wasn't that I ever *couldn't* really do anything. I mean, there were some things—like on weekend nights, when everybody was going out, I just didn't go out. Yet, I worked. I still went to school. But I *didn't* enjoy anything. It was just like a chore, trying to force myself to do these things. So that's when I decided to get help, and I was referred to PASS by my county mental health association.

The PASS program gave me some new tools to work with. Like the relaxation tape and learning how the body works and realizing that you're not the "only one" this is happening to. Dr. Weekes's book was also very helpful. My sister had the same problem with panic attacks, and she read Dr. Weekes's book, then she gave it to me. So I started reading it. To me, the most comforting thing was learning that the panic attacks never get any worse, that they can only go so far. And also, that you *do* have control over them.

I began to apply Dr. Weekes's four principles. I'd remember how she'd say, "Face, do not run away." That means just face it, just relax with it. Don't say, "Oh, my gosh, what's happening . . . ?!!" Don't think about it at all—float past it.

It was very helpful, too, when I learned about the home bases. It's funny, because that was how I would feel—when I'd go someplace, I always used to feel safe in my car. It was like my home base, although I never called it that before. So there were many things I found useful. Like realizing that everybody gets edgy at times about different things. So if I was edgy one day, I'd say to myself, "Well, don't put too much weight on it because it's only one day." A lot of pressure is off me now because I don't have to have things "perfect" all the time.

What I also found helpful was the advice I got from my counselor about the "worry hour"—to put all my worries into that one time-slot during the day. Because if you think about something all day long, it can get you crazy. This way, I knew I could worry about my problem a little later, whatever it was. So it definitely helped. It shortened my "worry time."

My biggest fear used to be going away places and staying overnight. Now, I can pretty much go anywhere. I own a boat, and it makes me feel good when I think that I'm able to go out on that boat and I'm able to handle things by myself. You know, being in a boat is quite different from being in a car. In a car, you can go out to make a phone call if you need help, or you can always pull over to the side of the road. But in a boat, you can't do that. My boat doesn't come equipped with a ship-to-shore radio. And even the driving is different; it's not like driving a car. There's a lot of maneuvering you have to do.

But I enjoy boating very much. I live on Long Island and I'm near the water. The couple of times I went boating before was with different guys that I went out with. And then one day, I just decided to buy a boat for myself. I took the course that the Coast Guard offers. They tell you about all the things you have to know, like the waterways, how to read the markers, the channels, and the mechanical things on the boat. It was like a regular college semester, but in Adult Ed. There were a lot of married couples in my class, and a lot of older people; I was the only single girl in my class.

I really enjoy my involvement with the boat. I think it's a good idea to keep busy with something you really like. It keeps your mind off yourself.

Scott's Story

Since I put this program into effect, there have been enormous changes in my life. I'm able to work again. I go into stores. I can go up to the doctor's office. And there's a general feeling of well-being. Before, I felt like—"What's the use of going on like this?" At one point, things were so bad that I even contemplated suicide! I thought it was hopeless because I'd been that way for so long—thirteen years! (It started when I was about twenty-one—and I'm thirty-four now.) Finally, it got to the point when three or four months before I started the PASS program, I was literally housebound!

The series of events that led to my becoming housebound and having thoughts of suicide were these: I lost my job because of the constant panic attacks. I had totally run out of money, and I decided I had to go out and get a job. I live in a small town and there aren't many jobs available. So I went to a large city nearby to look for work. But as I traveled, I found it harder and harder to get out of my car. (Instead of being housebound, I was becoming carbound!) It was so hard even to go to a gas station to get gas. But I had to do it, so I did. I'd wait around in my car until it got dark and not many people were there, and then I'd go up and get gas.

When I came back to my hometown, jobless, I moved in with my parents. (I'm single.) And I more or less stayed around the house, doing nothing and being miserable. Things just got worse and worse. And, after a while, I just became housebound. I couldn't go anywhere. Then, the bank called up to say that they were going to repossess my car for nonpayment. So that spurred me to get some help somewhere. A doctor came to the house and he prescribed Xanax, and that didn't do any good. He doubled the dosage, but it still didn't do any good. Finally, he gave me massive doses of Librium, twenty-five milligrams three times a day. With that, I was able to go to the doctor's office regularly, but that was about it.

Just by chance, I picked up a magazine and saw an article about panic attacks—and they mentioned PASS. I joined immediately. At that point, I was willing to do anything at all that might help me. I loved sugar, sweets, chocolate and pop—things like that—but I just dropped them. I think if my counselor had told me to cut off my left arm to get better, I would have done it. I wanted to change so badly, I would have done anything!

At about this time, I met a man who worked at the bank (the one that was going to repossess my car), and who later became my good friend. He took me aside and asked me what exactly was the problem. I leveled with him; I told him about the panic attacks. He told me he understood perfectly because a while back, he himself had suffered from panic attacks. Looking at him, so self-assured, so confident, and a bank officer, I suddenly felt that I, too, could regain my confidence and self-esteem. This man recommended that I read certain books, like Wayne Dyer's book *Pulling Your Own Strings* (HarperCollins, 1991)—which I did. (It's an excellent book and I reread it all the time.)

From what this man said, and from the books I've read since, I developed a new attitude that I call "aggressive friendliness." I simply radiate, all around me, friendliness combined with enthusiasm. And believe me, it really works! Whenever I'd feel intimidated by someone, I would just walk up to him, hold out my hand, and give that person an enthusiastic greeting. An amazing thing would happen: I would no longer feel intimidated by that person! For example, there was this man I knew in my town, and he always used to give me problems. So, one day, I spotted him in the street. I pulled my car up to the curb, parked, and got out of my car. I called his name, walked over, put my hand on his shoulder and said, "How are you?" in a loud, friendly voice. And as I shook his hand, I could feel *him* shaking!

Another attitude I adopted is "Who the hell cares?" I'd walk into a store—and if I'd start to have a panic attack, big deal! I didn't care. If people noticed and got a kick out of it—well, that was *their* problem, not mine. So the panic attacks were cured almost overnight, so to speak.

When I was younger, I used to drink like mad to cover up my nervousness. I used to feel better when I was "loaded." So I gradually became a heavy drinker—and I did this for many years. But now I stopped drinking altogether. How did I stop? After I started looking for a job and couldn't find any and I had to move in with my parents, I couldn't drink anymore. I couldn't get "loaded" in front of them—and I wasn't able to go to a bar. So I was, in a way, forced to stop. I actually had withdrawal symptoms. But, in a way, it was good it happened—now I don't need a drink to make me feel good. There are far better ways—like good food, exercise and relaxation.

Sharon's Story

I've been feeling fine. I've been eating well since I've been on the PASS program, but I'm especially careful with my diet now because I'm expecting twins in two more months!

Now that I'm home, I have more time to prepare better foods. When I was working, I'd have to get up early and we'd get home kind of late, so it was a lot harder getting good meals together. But now that I'm home, I can spend more time in the kitchen.

I had a thyroid problem at one time, and that, I believe, contributed to my having panic attacks. But I don't have a thyroid problem anymore—not since they treated this condition with radioactive iodine.

I used to worry a lot about my health. I'd be thinking about illnesses and disaster all the time. I used to feel panicky over long periods of time. I found it difficult to go to work, and I had a problem sleeping. I used to have feelings of unreality. I couldn't go places without fearing I'd get a panic attack there.

Thank God I don't think that anymore! How did I change? I think I learned just to ignore those panicky feelings. What helped me most was just realizing that other people have these problems, too, and that it really wasn't anything. I found that when you turn your attention away from yourself, those feelings really go away. In fact, I heard on the radio—they had this psychologist on, I think it was Dr. David Viscott. Anyhow, this woman called and she said she had these feelings of panic and she described it. She was afraid of dying. And he said, "Look, you're afraid of dying. But you're only going to die once—and it's not your time to die now." That's all it is. And that's how I've been looking at it, too. So these feelings don't bother me much, anymore.

I found out that in many situations, you have to just *do* the thing you're afraid of, and the fear goes away. Often, the anticipation is a lot worse than what actually happens. For instance: I used to be frightened about any kind of public speaking. But then, at work, I was promoted to a position where this was mainly my job—to speak before people. I wanted this promotion—and yet I didn't want it, because I had to hold meetings, and so on.

But I *did* get the promotion. And right off the bat, they told me I had to instruct a class of about thirty people, whom I didn't even know! These were trainees—new people who were hired. (I worked for a federal agency and they would hire a lot of people at once; there was a high turnover in this particular job.) They told me I had to do it. I had no choice. I wasn't about to quit my job.

Well, for several days, I felt terrible. I just couldn't help thinking about it. I was afraid. What if something happened to me in front of these people? On my first day on the new job, I got up there and I "shook." But to me, I sounded a lot worse than I must have come off. Because afterward, people were saying to me, "You were really very helpful"; "You were the best instructor I ever had"; and "We really understand what you were talking about." So, after one or two times, it became so easy. After a while, speaking before a group became so second nature to me; I looked forward to it!

Instead of thinking so much about myself and what other people were thinking about me, I started to think: Look, what's the difference—and if they don't like me, who cares? I also put myself in the other position, like I'm in the audience, listening to a lecture. I remembered how I felt, listening to a speech and thinking how the other person up there came off sounding so good. Then, I'd find out afterward how nervous they were. And I couldn't imagine why, they sounded so confident and secure. And I didn't think any less of them for being nervous. I didn't ridicule them. Nobody sat there and laughed. So when I was on the other side, speaking, I imagined people were thinking of me the same way.

It's the same with panicky feelings. You can say to yourself, it's really nothing and you play it down and it goes away. I don't believe in looking into everything that you do and making too much out of it. I'm not doing that anymore.

Tracy's Story

I had a problem with recurrent panic attacks for ten years. My dream was to be free of the panic attacks and be able to enjoy more of my life.

I joined the PASS program because I read an article in my

local newspaper about how a woman was helped through this program. When I first began the program, I found that it involved a great deal of eating—very much more than I was accustomed to. The decaffeinated coffee in the morning disturbed me because I felt I couldn't "get going" without that little bit of caffeine in the morning. But I soon got used to doing without it. Also, the vitamins and amounts of food—I just wasn't used to eating a lot. But my counselor helped me out with the food plan. I stopped smoking, too, as a result of this program, and the interesting thing about it is my weight stayed the same! My weight is absolutely normal. The reason it remained the same was because I compensated for the extra food by doing more exercise, more walking. Now I like the eating and exercise habits I acquired. To this day, I find I'm putting something in my mouth every three or three and a half hours. Before, I could go from breakfast or even skip breakfast altogether and not eat until, say, one in the afternoon. Now, I go munching along with my snacks. I feel better when I'm doing this. I don't know if it's psychological or not, but I just do feel better.

What things can I do now that I wasn't able to before? I can food-shop alone. I can go into any shopping mall by myself. I can get into my car and drive wherever I want to go. I feel free! Those were the things I couldn't do before. Of course, I worked even before I took this course. But my life is so much better now—it's freer and easier. Before the program, every time I stepped out the door, I would ask myself, "Will I be all right? How will I feel?" Now, I go out the door and say "I'm fine!" And I get in the car and I'm involved in where I'm going and what I'm doing. If I'm at a mall—and many times this goes through my mind—I remember the panic attacks. But I just slow down, do the breathing exercises and I get involved in what I'm looking at. I stop to check a rack out, check sizes, and so on. It passes, and I continue. Many times, while food-shopping, before the program, I'd buy six things—and leave them in the store and run out. Or I'd travel half the distance to someplace and have to turn back home.

I must tell you about this. A short while after I began the program, we had a very big crisis—my husband suffered a heart attack. I was literally forced to drive on the highway, by myself, in order to get to the hospital to see him. But I put to use all the methods I learned from the program. I thought that was quite an achievement, being able to do that. When my husband was finally out of the hospital and recovering, his doctor told us he wanted him to exercise, to walk. He suggested that he walk in the mall because it has a controlled temperature there. Well, that was so traumatic for me. When the doctor said this is what he had to do, I thought I'd die. I said to myself, "I can't do this—malls—forget about it!" But then I had a big talk with myself. I said, "Look. You're eating correctly now; you're exercising, you're doing the relaxation. You're going to try this—because *he needs you!*" And, of course, my husband was nervous, too, because this was only three weeks after it happened, and he was not quite himself yet. But since I knew he needed me now, I went to the mall. We walked past three or four stores, and I looked at him and I smiled and I said, "This is fun—and I can do it." So this program came along just at the right time. I put it all to use, all the information I got.

My husband's doctor told him to walk a half-mile, then one mile; now, we walk three miles a day. My husband is now on pretty much the same foods I'm eating, so that makes it a lot easier for me. He's got a stressful job, which he doesn't allow to get to him anymore. So we do these things together. We eat the same kinds of food and we exercise, we walk together. I feel it's such a small price to pay for what we've gained. These are the good things that have developed.

I feel now that I really want to pass on this help. I want to help others as I've been helped. So I'm in training now to be a counselor for PASS. The counselor I had was so terrific and so sincere—I admire her very much. I used to think, "If I ever get to be as well as she is, I want to do this, too." Well, now I'm at that point.

Vivian's Story

Panic attacks were a part of my life for five or six years, and the last couple of years were bad. But now, I just feel so good. I just feel like I'm a full person again. My relationship with my husband is much better now because we go and we do; I was afraid to go anywhere before. Now, he yells at me, Can't we stay home? I say no. Before, he'd want me to go out, but I wouldn't go. I couldn't go to a restaurant—I was afraid I'd have a panic attack. I would avoid a lot of situations. I became good at making up excuses: something always "hurt" me. But now, come a Saturday night or a Sunday, and I say to my husband, C'mon, let's go, let's get out of here. And now my husband sometimes says, Aw, not now, let's go later.

Like: Last week, my husband went to work and came home early. I didn't go to work that day. And—this would never have happened before—he looked at me and he said, "Do you want to go to Jersey?" Now, before, I would have made up every excuse possible not to go. But I just said, "All right." And I called up my sister and she said she was going to the beach club. Anyway, I put on my bathing suit and we got in the car. I couldn't believe it: We just got in the car and went! We went swimming at the club—it was beautiful there. And we came home. Now, I could never have done that before. Never in a million years. I never wanted to go to the beach—and I never wanted to go far. But this time, the next morning, I woke up my husband and said, "Let's go down to the beach again!"

So these are some of the things I'm doing now that I couldn't do before. I'm going away from the house—even overnight. When I went away to Cherry Hill, New Jersey, the other weekend, that was the first I'd been there in years—

and I loved it! I had such a good time, I couldn't believe it. I was there and nothing was bothering me. And the weekend before, we went to my other sister's house. It's like I can't wait to get up and go and get out of the house and do things. I feel great—so I'm just going.

How was it before I joined PASS? You know, it's hard to remember, I'm so far from it now! I used to be afraid to go out of the house before. I was afraid that if I had to run back home if I panicked, I wouldn't make it back. I had to always be within a certain distance, a safe distance. And I had to feel I was comfortable where I was going. So that, to me, was the best feeling—that I really went away and I didn't think of anything. And when I got home, I wanted to go back, so that's really great. I haven't had that feeling in years!

But back then, I couldn't do many things—like I couldn't go into an elevator alone. And even with somebody, I wasn't crazy about it. I used to get a panic attack every time I had to leave my house. I used to get random panic attacks, too—I'd be in a store, it would happen. I'd be driving, it would happen. For no reason, it would happen. Like I would just be sitting someplace, and I'd have one. Truthfully, my whole life then was just one big panic. I felt that no matter what I did, I'd get a panic attack. I couldn't work. And now I'm working full-time, every day, in my own business. I never even *thought* I could ever do what I'm doing. It's like my whole life is different. I just feel free. I don't feel that something is holding me back. I want to go and I just go. I mean, there are times that I still think about it—after all, it was in my life for so long—but I don't let it stop me.

Yvonne's Story

Till I was twenty, I was always a kind of "panicky type" person, but it never really bothered me. I didn't have panic attacks, but I had a tendency to get real panicky if I knew I was going to be away from home for a couple of nights without my mother. That used to make me real nervous. I just knew I didn't like it and therefore I avoided going away from home for a couple of days. Things got a little better when I was in my late teens. Then, I got married. I was married four years when I decided I wanted to have a baby. That's about the time it all really started—the panic attacks.

You see, I began dieting strenuously before I got pregnant. I wasn't too much overweight, but I felt I needed to lose a lot of weight. I knew I would gain a lot during pregnancy and I didn't want to wind up looking like a blimp. My method of losing weight consisted of not eating all day long; I wouldn't eat a thing, except maybe drink two or three pots of decaffeinated coffee, along with a lot of diet pop. I would have one meal at six o'clock. So I would literally starve all day long and "pig out" on the one meal. I lost about twenty pounds during that period, but I messed up my metabolism to the point where I would gain weight if I had more than seven hundred calories a day!

Just about that time, my mother died in a tragic accident. She'd been my "strong person" all along, and that was, oh, so hard for all of us. I don't know how I ever got through it. My youngest brother was twelve years old at the time and I decided to take him to live with us (I was already married then). I didn't realize it at the time, but this was another great big stress for me, because I was working at the time, too. Then, my boss asked me if I would be interested in a promotion, which would entail going to school. I said yes, because it meant a big promotion. But, boy, did I have a lot to learn! I was under constant pressure at work, and I was going to school. My husband couldn't help me too much at home because he worked at odd shifts. So I wound up having *three* full-time jobs: going to work, going to school, and doing the housework! And the way I abused my body, by not eating, by starving myself—all this set the stage for the panic attacks.

Well, I became pregnant and I had a little girl. (I only

gained fifteen pounds during the entire pregnancy.) But my daughter was one of those "ornery" babies that cried all the time, although nothing was wrong with her. She just wasn't a happy baby. And that endless crying just drove me berserk! Because I knew that after six weeks, I would be going back to work. I finally did go back to work, and a few months after that, I had my first real major panic attack.

I was out to lunch with my friends at work. We were sitting in a restaurant, in a booth, and someone mentioned a mutual friend of ours. She told us she heard that that person had a nervous breakdown. Well, I just fell apart! My heart started pounding, I felt faint, a great sense of impending doom came over me, and so on. Naturally, I overreacted because I myself had begun to suspect that I was having a nervous breakdown because I was having such a hard time coping with everything.

But things were dramatically turned around for me after I joined PASS. I started eating the right things. I realized that exercise, combined with the right diet, was going to get me to lose weight if I needed to. I was reassured. I finally knew what was wrong with me. I think the phrase "nervous breakdown" scared me the most. I used to have all kinds of visions about what was going to happen to me: Would I go into a mental institution? What would happen to my baby? And so on. But then, I finally got the attitude of: "So what?" And I think that once I started turning all those what-ifs into "So what?" it helped me tremendously. And I realized that things weren't that bad, anyhow. With this new attitude, I was also able to reduce some of the pressures in my life.

It was toward the end of the three-month counseling program that tragedy struck. By then, I had begun to feel a lot better. I could do a lot of things on my own; I could go pretty much anywhere I wanted to. Anyhow, I was going to work one day and I heard over the car radio that there was an accident at the company where I worked, a mining company. There was a fire in the mine and many miners were trapped underground! Nobody knew at the time whether they were alive or not. When I got to work, of course, nobody was working. The family members of the people who were trapped were already sitting in the offices, waiting for news. There was a tremendous rescue effort going on. So I was asked to man the phones, run the computer, and so on. The rescue efforts continued for days. One time, I was there for almost twenty-four hours. (I thought: Oh, this really is going to mess me up . . . I'm nervous as it is, and now I'm faced with death and grieving relatives and things like that.) I didn't know I could do it. But I did—I was able to help.

Where did I get my strength? I found that if my mind is not focused on me and what I'm experiencing and going through; if I'm able to focus on someone else or if I'm able to help other people—then that gives me the strength I need. It was a most valuable lesson to learn.

Teri's Story

I started having panic attacks about a year ago. I was in the car, and I was thinking about all that was going on in my life at the time: The doctors had found a cyst in my brain. My husband was sick. My grandfather had recently passed away. So I was thinking about illness and people dying.

The worst panic attack I ever had was when I was driving home from work one day. That was the day I found out my husband had hepatitis B, and I was thinking about that. I started shaking. I was in the middle of nowhere. There were no houses around, no stores. I was all alone in my own little world. It was *so* scary!

After that episode, I went to see a doctor. The doctor started me on medication, but the medication made me feel worse. So he sent me to a psychiatrist, who gave me a different medication. That made me feel even more nervous than I was at the beginning. Then I started seeing a psychologist.

One day, he gave me a book to read—it was *The Panic Attack Recovery Book*. And I started the telephone sessions, too.

Right away, I started eating better. I began exercising. I listened to the relaxation tape every day. But what helped me the most was my changed self-talk. Because as a result of the panic attacks, I had developed a lot of bad habits in my thinking. I used to try very hard not to think of a panic attack. Or I would think: "All those people, all those lights— Oh, I *know* I'm going to have a panic attack!" Or, when I started driving again and I'd come to a red light, I would think: "What if I feel panicky and I have to run out of the car?" But I don't do any of that now. Instead of overreacting, I've learned to underreact.

My first achievement after I started the program was to drive again. I had a new job to go to (I had quit my other job after I had that terrible panic attack in the car) and it was a big accomplishment to be able to drive there myself. Another major success was being able to attend a conference for my new job. Before, during the bad times, I wasn't able to be around a lot of people without getting panicky. Well, at the conference there were so many people all over the place— and they didn't even bother me! I never once thought of a panic attack. Another big adventure for me was being able to drive out to see my mother. To make the trip easier and to provide another "magnet" to help draw me to my destination, my counselor advised me to take along a little gift for my mother and to have her arrange a surprise for me. So that trip was a big success, too. We had a very nice time. (I gave my mother a pin and she gave me a gift of money.)

I have other good news, too. I had an MRI recently, and they found that the cyst in my brain, which was 1 centimeter, had not grown at all. The doctors now think it probably won't grow anymore and that maybe it's something I've had since birth. But they're still going to follow up with yearly check-ups. Everything else is fine—blood tests, thyroid, everything. My husband is doing great, too. A couple of months ago, he was in a car accident, but he's all right now. That was a scary time—when I heard about the accident and I had to go to the hospital by myself. But thank God it worked out fine.

I've had only one panic attack since I started the program. I was really stressed out—I worked sixty hours that week. I had stopped eating right and I'd stopped exercising because I was trying to get everything done. I only realized this *after* it happened. This time, I saw the panic attack as a warning sign. So I went back to my healthy routines, and now everything is okay.

What am I able to do now that I couldn't do before the program? I'm able to stay home by myself. Before, I couldn't stay home alone for five minutes. Two weeks ago, my husband had to go out of town on a business trip, but I was able to come home from work and stay by myself—no problem.

I've learned so much since I started the program. How to take better care of myself, how not to worry so much about everything going on around me. I learned better self-talk—I do that all the time now. I also think prayer is very important, feeling a connection to God. And the panic attacks also made me realize: Why worry so much when you can be enjoying your life? Nobody knows how long we'll be here, so it's important to be happy while we are here.

Lara's Story

Just before I graduated from college, I started to get panic attacks. At the time, I didn't know what they were. When I came home from school, I started interviewing for jobs almost immediately. I began having panic attacks on the train on the way to the interview. One was a major, major panic attack. It was so bad that my sister, who happened to be with me because she had to go into the city that day too, had to tell the conductor about me, and they were able to re-route the train to a nearby station so I could get off. It was a terrible experience, and after that I stopped traveling on trains. Then I started to have panic attacks just doing little things, like going to a store. I stopped doing that, too. Eventually I didn't want to leave the house at all. The "what-ifs" snowballed and I was practically crazed with anxiety. It got to the point where I wouldn't even let my *mother* leave the house because she was my "safe" person. That was a horrible time for my family.

After about six weeks, my mother called in a professional and she started to help me get out of the house. Little by little, I began reaching out again. I called up my friends. I wasn't working; I was seeing a therapist, and I functioned as best I could.

A few months later, it was my birthday, and my "then" boyfriend brought me a present. It was *The Panic Attack Recovery Book*. I leafed through the book and saw all those stories in the back. I started to read them. I was so impressed because I could see myself in them. I couldn't wait to call PASS-Group, I was so eager to start the phone counseling. I began to make big changes in my lifestyle and I also started to do all kinds of things that were challenging. I did it because I had a ferocious craving to rid myself of those panic attacks. I began deliberately to put myself into situations that would cause me to panic, so that I could desensitize myself.

There's one experience I'll never forget because it encompassed three of my biggest fears: getting on a train; being in New York City; and being in a closed-in place with lots of people. I was with my sister and my best friend, and we went to the city to see a Broadway show. Afterward, we had to go uptown in Manhattan. We could have taken a cab or we could have walked. But I insisted that we take the subway. And not the local train either, where I could easily get off at the next station if I felt a panic attack coming on. I wanted to take the express train, where I couldn't get off even if I wanted to. I clearly remember being at the station, standing inside the open door of the express train and seeing the local train and its open doors right across the platform. We could easily have crossed over and gone on the local. My girlfriend and my sister said, "Let's take the local." I said, "Absolutely not; we're taking the express." They kept asking me, "Are you sure? Are you sure?" But I insisted; I made the decision to stay on the express train. And for me—a person who had for so long avoided any place that might bring on a panic attack—this was an amazing thing to do. But I knew this was a grand opportunity for me to confront my fears. After all, I had my sister and my best friend with me. I just *had* to do it then and there.

Anyhow, after that train ride, I was ecstatic. I was tickled pink. It had been so difficult for me—and yet I did it!

To sum up where I am in my life today: I've been completely panic-free for about four years now. I have my own apartment. I go, I travel, I do everything. I even drove cross-country a while ago. What's different now is that I really take good care of myself. I listen to my body. When I'm hungry, I eat. I exercise regularly. When I'm tired, I rest right away; I don't let myself get overtired. I have a very good social life. I have a wonderful boyfriend. I work full-time. I have a very interesting job—I work in a hospital, in the ER—and I commute to work every day, an hour each way. The interesting thing is that I work in such a chaotic atmosphere, and yet I feel no fear. In fact, people come in all the time, panicked and afraid—they've been in accidents and what-not—and there I am, soothing and calming *them!*

I'm so honored to contribute my story to the book. Because I know what it's like to be caught in the throes of fear, and I want to tell you that there *is* a way out. Panic attacks are not forever. With the right approach, you *can* recover!

Mary's Story

I've had panic attacks for many years. They started when I was in my twenties. The doctors back then didn't know about panic attacks. They told me it was "just nerves" and they gave me a small dose of phenobarbital, which was the only thing they could offer in those days. But that didn't help much. Besides, I didn't want to continue taking it because I'm a nurse and I knew it was a barbiturate and addictive. Anyway, I continued to have panic attacks for quite some time, and somehow I managed without medication. I was always a bit embarrassed about having panic attacks. When I'd try and talk to someone about them—well, actually, I'd tiptoe around the subject—people didn't know what I was talking about. My friends wanted to be helpful, but they just didn't understand.

My husband was very ill for quite some time before he died. It was such a stressful situation and the panic attacks surfaced again, full-force. I went to see a psychologist, who advised me to go into rehab for a week. I didn't want to do that because I didn't feel it was right for me. So I just "limped along" as best I could. But after my husband died, I was so lonely. I had this great big house, and there I was, all by myself. Sure, I had old friends, and they were very good friends too, but I was still very lonely. My son, who lives on the east coast, wanted me to sell the house and move closer to him. In a way, I wanted very much to do that. But I also wanted to stay in the town I was used to, among my familiar friends. So it was a very traumatic time for me. All my symptoms were magnified tenfold.

About that time I heard of PASS-Group. There was an article about it in *RN Magazine*. I joined the program. Now I had someone to talk to, someone who I knew would understand my problem. One thing my counselor, Shirley, told me stuck with me. I should try not to see myself as being alone, but, rather, as being my own person, my own boss. That shift in viewpoint helped me so much. It made me realize how many resources I actually had within myself. Shirley also talked about *her* move to a new town and how she had made new friends there and created a good social life for herself.

So I began to think more about the possibility of moving, seeing it as a step toward a better future. Anyhow, as soon as I felt up to it (I had the flu that winter), I decided to visit my son and his family. I had a wonderful time there and my son accompanied me back home. I was greeted by friends and I felt very happy.

Then, for a number of reasons, I decided to make the move. Shirley encouraged me to join a senior center once I got to the new town, and that's what I did. At first, I felt apprehensive and very out of place. But the administrator of that center was so nice. She took me around and introduced me to everyone, and they all seemed happy I was with them. So that went very well. I do crafts, and that's what they were doing too—making crafts and selling them and then using the money to go on trips. I liked the people there and I became involved with that group. And then I got interested in the church, too. I also heard of another senior group in town. Once a week they meet for a pot luck dinner, and I joined that, too. I'm active in my clubs, and I have a wonderful social life here. I also see my son and my daughter-in-law and my grandchildren. I still have my friends from back home, whom I recently visited. So I feel very blessed and very content with my life now.

I've found this to be a wonderful strategy when moving to a new place: Find a club you can join, and then, within that club, you can always find more personal friends. But you have to go with a positive attitude. I kept saying to myself: "Go—it's going to be good for you." And that's the way it turned out to be.

Another thing that I believe is helpful, especially for an older person, is to have a pet. Something that loves you and that you have to take care of. Then you don't think about yourself all the time. I have three dogs in my home. Before they came to me, these animals were so abused and neglected. But I nursed them back to health and now they're fine and they give me so much pleasure.

Susan's Story

I used to suffer from panic attacks for many years. They seemed to come on at random. I would be minding my own business, and suddenly, out of the blue, I'd be zapped by a dreadful feeling, an overwhelming feeling of panic. I used to expend so much energy fighting the panic attacks—or just plain trying to get through the day. And yet I knew if I didn't make myself do things, I'd get to the point where fear would rule my life and I'd become housebound. And I certainly didn't want that. So I used to go places, but with trepidation.

I never stopped looking for answers. I always wanted to know: What was causing these panic attacks? Because I felt if I knew that, I'd be able to do something about them.

Well, finally I got my answers. I came across Dr. Claire Weekes's books, in which she talks about not fighting the panic attacks and not adding additional fear, like, "Oh, my goodness, what's happening to me?" I learned that the panic attacks can be triggered by stress and being run-down. I joined the PASS Program, and for the first time, learned the effect my diet was having on the panic attacks.

My diet was terrible. Yet if you'd asked me at the time, I would have said, "Oh, I'm eating well." For breakfast, I'd grab a doughnut and two or three cups of coffee on my way to work. Then, about ten o'clock I'd get weak and shaky, so I'd grab another doughnut and maybe have a Coke with it. For dinner, there'd be meat and potatoes, and there was always a rich, gooey dessert afterward. I don't know why I didn't gain a lot of weight in those days, but I didn't. Anyway, once I corrected my diet and started to eat sensibly and at frequent intervals, it made a tremendous difference in the way I felt.

I also happened to be taking a course in cognitive psychology that enabled me to unravel some of the faulty thinking that contributed to my panic attacks. For instance, whenever I had to do anything, I'd always anticipate disaster. My first thoughts would be: "What if I get a panic attack? What if this, what if that . . . ?" I had a number of "Aha" experiences in class. One was when we talked about the "shoulds" and the "oughts" and the "shame-on-you upbringing" most of us had. The important lesson I got out of that was to accept myself as I am. To allow myself to be imperfect. I began to recognize that being imperfect didn't make me a failure.

Before that, I'd always been ashamed of having panic attacks. I spent a lot of effort in keeping people from knowing that I had panic attacks. But then I began to see my situation in a new light. I realized: Hey, rather than be ashamed of having panic attacks, I could congratulate myself for having lived as normal a life as I had. I was married; I had raised three wonderful children; I was going back to school to get my Bachelor of Fine Arts—I was doing a lot of things *despite* the panic attacks.

So bit by bit, I began to recover. I changed my lifestyle, my thinking. And I finally conquered the panic attacks. In fact, it's hard to remember them—it's like they happened to a different person.

How am I today? Terrific! I'm working—I have a wonderful job (I've been there a few years now). I'm in charge of educational operations for my organization. As part of my job, I often give talks to schoolchildren, to women's groups, and so on. And I love doing that. I'm so happy that I can do so many interesting and wonderful things now. It's such a far cry from the panic-person I used to be.

Shirley Swede's Story

I guess my story is not so very different from many others. For years I used to have panic attacks that seemed to come out of nowhere—or so I thought. They got worse when I was in my thirties. I was pretty high-strung in those days, and I worried a lot. I'd go to doctors, but they never found anything wrong. One thing, though: I never became homebound. I'd have panic attacks in the subways. On the street. Many times in restaurants. But I kept going. It never occurred to me not to go—although I admit there were a few rare days when I just couldn't make myself open that front door.

In addition to panic attacks, I remember having a lot of phobias. Some I developed in childhood; others, later. At various times, I had a fear of heights, crowds, dogs, spiders, escalators, driving, flying, public speaking—you name it. But I'm happy to report: Hooray! I conquered them all!

How? Some, like the fear of escalators, I overcame simply by thinking: "Hey, others are doing it. Let me try, too." On escalators I feared I wouldn't be able to jump off in time and my foot would get caught in the machinery. But I tried it and found that I *could* do it safely. I overcame the spider phobia after reading *Charlotte's Web* to my daughter. Some of my fears—like flying or driving—were a lot more resistant, but eventually I demolished them, too. And in the process I discovered something interesting about phobias: Bravery begets bravery. The courage you build up in one area carries over to other areas as well.

How did I recover from panic disorder?

Well, a number of things came together over a relatively short time. I never connected these events or thought they had anything to do with panic attacks until much later. I had enrolled in nursing school and we had to take a class in nutrition. This gave me the knowledge and incentive to greatly improve my diet. I started an exercise program after a handsome doctor, who examined me all over, told me I was too flabby—how embarrassing! And just about this time, my dentist taught me how to relax so he could begin to work on my teeth.

Another event was also relevant, although I didn't know it at the time. One day, I was in the library while a lecture was going on in another room. I stopped to listen and heard the lecturer tell the audience that we have choices in life: it's not the circumstances that determine our reaction; rather, it's the way we *interpret* the events that shapes our reaction. What an eye-opener *that* was! I can still remember the excitement I felt when I first heard those words, because they seemed to open up new possibilities for me. Before that, I thought that if a negative thing happened to you, or if somebody didn't love you, then of course you'd have to react negatively or be unhappy. I believed such things were automatic and that you didn't have a choice.

After a while, I noticed something remarkable happening to me: My intense nervousness diminished, and the panic attacks that had bothered me for so long seemed to abate. I was involved with school and other things, and I was feeling much better. Still, in the back of my mind, I wondered about the panic attacks. What kind of sickness could this be? What could the panic attacks mean? And would they come back again full-force?

One night, as I was getting ready for bed, I put on the radio and I heard someone give a very graphic description of a panic attack. I couldn't believe it! This person on the air was talking about *me*. It was Dr. Claire Weekes from Australia, who had come to this country on a book tour. The very next day I bought her book *Hope and Help For Your Nerves,* (Hawthorne, 1969) and in it I found the missing piece of the puzzle. Panic attacks, she wrote, are common. They're not dangerous. They're not life threatening. They're not a fore-runner of some major disease.

Whew! In that case, why worry about them? And that thought was the beginning of my true recovery.

Not long afterward, I was ready—and eager—to put my experience in overcoming panic attacks and phobias to good use. I wanted the personal satisfaction of turning all those minuses into pluses. In 1981, I founded PASS-Group, Inc., and I've been involved with this organization ever since.

Looking back now, I'm not sorry I had panic attacks. In fact, I'm glad I did. Because in the process of recovering I learned some very valuable lessons about how to live a healthier and happier life. And being able to help so many others recover has brought me immense joy.

Books We Recommend

Dr. Kenneth Cooper's Antioxidant Revolution, by Kenneth H. Cooper. Thomas Nelson, 1997.

Regaining the Power of Youth at Any Age, by Kenneth H. Cooper. Thomas Nelson, 1999.

Connect, by Edward M. Hallowell, M.D. Pantheon Books, 1999.

Feel the Fear—And Do It Anyway, by Susan Jeffers, Ph.D. Fawcett Colombine, 1987.

The Resolution Diet, by David Heber, M.D. Avery Publishing Group, 1999.

Strong Women Stay Young, by Miriam E. Nelson, Ph.D., and Sarah Wernick. Bantam Books, 1997.

TO ORDER

The PASS-Group Relaxation Tape.....................$11.50
The Exercise Game...6.50

Prices include shipping & handling. Please send check or M.O. to

PASS-Group, Inc.
6 Mahogany Drive
Williamsville, NY 14221

PERSONAL COUNSELING

To augment this book with personal telephone counseling, call PASS-Group, Inc., at:
(716) 689-4399

Index

PASS program (*cont.*)
  diet, 49–72
  exercise, 87–95
  imagination, 108–118
  interrelatedness of elements in, 71–72
  preparing for, *see* Preparing for PASS program
  relaxation, 73–86
  social support, 119–132
  spiritual values, 133–39
Patience, 158–60
Pavlov, Ivan, 79, 110
Peace from Nervous Suffering (Weekes), 35
Perfectionism, 41–42, 155
Phobias, 6, 43
  self-help groups, 131–32
Pituitary gland, 10
Planning to make a trip, 147, 152–55
Pleasurable tie-ins, 146–47, 152–55
Pleasure islands, 33–34
Positive energy in a group, 132
Positive thoughts, *see* Attitude
Potato salad recipe, 68
Potatoes, 60, 68
Poultry, 54, 55, 58, 67
Practicing relaxation, 84
Premenstrual syndrome (PMS), 27, 30
Preparing for PASS program, 31–45

Pretending, 108–10, 110–13
Principles for easy meal preparation, 61–64
Problem-solving methods, 38–40
Processed foods, 54, 64
  food additives, 57
Protein, 53, 55, 67
Prototype recipes, 65–69
Psychosis, 43, 113
Pulse rate, 91

QR (Quieting Reflex), 76–78, 155, 182

Reader's Digest, 171
Reading list, recommended, 248
Recipes:
  baked vegetables, 67
  cinnamon-walnut "coffee cake," 69
  fruit or vegetable pie, 66
  prototype, 65
  salad, 68
  vegetable soup, 69
Recovering from panic disorder, 5
  anticipatory anxiety, 156–66
  dealing with the unknown, 167–72
  gaining confidence by doing, 173–88